cook's library
Soups

cook's library
Soups

p

This is a Parragon Book
This edition published in 2003

Parragon
Queen Street House
4 Queen Street
Bath BA1 1HE, UK

ISBN: 0-75258-753-6

Printed in China

NOTE

This book uses metric and imperial measurements. Follow the same
units of measurement throughout; do not mix metric and imperial.
All spoon measurements are level: teaspoons are assumed to be 5 ml,
and tablespoons are assumed to be 15 ml. Unless otherwise stated,
milk is assumed to be full fat, eggs and individual vegetables such as
potatoes are medium, and pepper is freshly ground black pepper.

The times given for each recipe are an approximate guide only because
the preparation times may differ according to the techniques used by
different people and the cooking times may vary as a result of the type
of oven used. The preparation times include chilling and marinating
times, where appropriate.

Recipes using raw or very lightly cooked eggs should be avoided
by infants, the elderly, pregnant women, convalescents and anyone
suffering from an illness.

Contents

Introduction

Soup is one of the most fundamental forms of food. Its traditions go back to the earliest days of civilised man with the advent of fire. It remains a favourite source of nourishment and pleasure today and home-made soup has become a special treat.

The benefits of soup are numerous. It is nutritious, satisfying to eat and generally lean. It is economical to make, especially using abundant seasonal produce, but even expensive ingredients like lobster go further when made into soups.

Making soup can be a very creative endeavour, as satisfying for the cook as the recipients. Practice hones skills and promotes confidence. This book offers an array of different styles of soup, using a variety of ingredients and techniques. Consider the recipes as a framework of proportions, and experiment with alternative ingredients if you wish.

Ingredients

Soups are as good as the ingredients in them. While leftovers have traditionally been a springboard for creativity in soup-making, and may certainly provide useful components, fresh ingredients at their peak provide optimum nutritional benefits and taste. Water is the most basic ingredient for soup. Even stock is essentially flavoured water. Many soups taste best made with water, as the pure flavours are highlighted – this is especially true of vegetable soups.

Some soups make their own stock during the cooking process. Others call for stock as an ingredient. This can be home-made, bought ready-made, made up from stock cubes, powder or liquid stock base, or canned consommé or clear broth. It is useful to know how to make stock, as home-made is more economical and normally has superior flavour.

Equipment

Soup-making requires little in the way of basic equipment. A good knife or two and a large saucepan with a lid are essential. A stock pot or soup kettle, or a large cast-iron casserole, is also useful. Other things needed to expedite your efforts are probably already in your kitchen – a cutting board, colander, sieves, vegetable peeler, scissors, ladle, spoons. A fat separator or de-greasing jug is helpful, as is a large measuring container.

A wide range of specialised equipment is available, but not necessarily essential for making soups. For puréeing soups, the various options produce differing results. A food mill, the most economical choice, will do the basic job of producing relatively smooth soups and it also sieves at the same time. For the smoothest and best texture, nothing beats a blender. A food processor may be used for chopping and slicing ingredients as well as for puréeing cooked soups, so it performs a variety of functions. A hand-held blender can purée right in the saucepan, as long as the depth of liquid is appropriate.

These pieces of equipment may each have a role to play in soup-making, but it's best to experiment first and see what you really need for the soups you like to make before investing. For most people, there is no need for a battery of equipment. Always follow manufacturer's instructions and recommendations for safe operation of electric appliances.

Stock-making

Making stock is easy. After getting it under way, it requires little attention, just time. You can save stock ingredients in the freezer until you need them: chicken carcasses, giblets, necks, backs and trimmings; scraps and bones from meat roasts; vegetable trimmings such as leek greens, celery leaves and stems, mushroom stalks, pieces of carrot and unused onion halves.

Recipes appear throughout the book using Fish Stock (see page 14), Beef Stock (see page 15), Chicken Stock (see page 14) and Vegetable Stock (see page 14). The following general points cover the basic techniques of stock-making.

Fresh ingredients are determined by the kind of stock you want. Chicken or turkey wings are inexpensive and provide excellent flavour for poultry stock. Veal bones give more flavour than beef and pork bones lend sweetness to the stock. Lamb or ham bones are not suitable for a general purpose meat stock, as the flavours are too pronounced, but can make delicious stocks when their flavours are appropriate, such as ham stock for split pea or bean soup. Aromatic vegetables – carrot, onion, leek, garlic, for instance – are almost always included in stock. Strongly flavoured vegetables like cabbage or swede should be used sparingly, as the stock produced would be unsuitable for delicate soups. Avoid dark leafy greens as they tend to make stock murky.

Except when a pale, delicate stock is wanted, browning the main ingredients first, either by roasting or frying, adds colour and richer flavour to the stock. Adding a roast chicken carcass or two is an easy way to do this.

Use cold water to make stock; it helps extract impurities. For a flavourful stock, keep the amount of water in proportion to the ingredients, which should be covered by about 5 cm / 2 inches. Skim off the scum or foam that rises to the surface as stock is heated, as it contains impurities that can make stock cloudy. Cook stock uncovered and do not allow it to boil at any point or fat may be incorporated into the liquid, unable to be removed.

Stock needs slow cooking over a low heat. Beef or meat stock takes 4–6 hours to extract maximum flavour, chicken or other poultry stock 2–3 hours. Fish stock only requires about half an hour of cooking.

Remove the fat from stock before using. The easiest way to do this is to refrigerate it, allowing the fat to congeal, then lift off the fat. If time is short, use a fat separator (a jug with the spout at the bottom) to remove the fat from warm stock, or spoon off the fat, although that is not nearly as effective as the other methods.

For greater flavour, stock can be reduced – cooked slowly, uncovered, to reduce and concentrate it. This procedure may also be useful to reduce the volume for storage. Stock keeps refrigerated for about 3 days or frozen for several months.

Serving soup

Soup is more flexible in terms of portions than many other foods. In this book a range of servings may be indicated, as a soup will provide more servings as a starter than as the focus of a meal. Starter portions range from 225 ml/8 fl oz for a very rich soup to 350 ml/12 fl oz; main course portions from 400 ml/14 fl oz to about 600 ml/1 pint.

Soup is a perfect food for almost any occasion, from the most casual to the very formal. It can set the tone for the rest of a meal or be the meal itself. It brings satisfaction to those who make it as well as those who eat it and nourishes both the body and the soul.

Basic Recipes

These recipes form the basis of several of the dishes contained throughout this book. Many of these basic recipes can be made in advance and stored in the refrigerator until required.

Fresh Chicken Stock

MAKES
1.75 LITRES/3 PINTS

1 kg/2 lb 4 oz chicken, skinned
2 celery sticks, chopped
1 onion, sliced
2 carrots, chopped
1 garlic clove
a few fresh parsley sprigs
2 litres/3½ pints water
salt and pepper

1 Place all the ingredients in a large saucepan and bring to the boil.

2 Skim away any surface scum using a large flat spoon. Reduce the heat to a gentle simmer, partially cover and cook for 2 hours. Leave to cool.

3 Line a sieve with clean muslin and place over a large jug or bowl. Pour the stock through the sieve. The cooked chicken can be used in another recipe. Discard the other solids. Cover the stock and chill.

4 Skim away any surface fat before using. Store in the refrigerator for up to 3 days, or freeze in small batches until required.

Fresh Vegetable Stock

MAKES
1.75 LITRES/3 PINTS

1 large onion, sliced
1 large carrot, chopped
1 celery stick , chopped
2 garlic cloves
1 dried bay leaf
a few fresh parsley sprigs
pinch of grated nutmeg
2 litres/3½ pints water
salt and pepper

1 Place all the ingredients in a large saucepan and bring to the boil.

2 Skim away any surface scum using a large flat spoon. Reduce the heat to a gentle simmer, partially cover and cook for 45 minutes. Leave to cool.

3 Line a sieve with clean muslin and place over a large jug or bowl. Pour the stock through the sieve. Discard the solids.

4 Cover the stock and store in the refrigerator for up to 3 days, or freeze in small batches until required.

Fresh Fish Stock

MAKES
1.75 LITRES/3 PINTS

1 kg/2 lb 4 oz white fish bones, heads and scraps
1 large onion, chopped
2 carrots, chopped
2 celery sticks, chopped
½ tsp black peppercorns
½ tsp grated lemon rind
a few fresh parsley sprigs
2 litres/3½ pints water
salt and pepper

1 Rinse the fish trimmings in cold water and place in a large saucepan with all the other ingredients. Bring to the boil.

2 Skim away any surface scum using a large flat spoon. Reduce the heat to a gentle simmer, partially cover and cook for 30 minutes. Leave to cool.

3 Line a sieve with clean muslin and place over a large jug or bowl. Pour the stock through the sieve. Discard the solids.

4 Cover the stock and store in the refrigerator for up to 3 days, or freeze in small batches until required.

Fresh Beef Stock

MAKES
1.75 LITRES/3 PINTS

about 1 kg/2 lb 4 oz bones from a cooked
joint or raw chopped beef
2 onions, studded with 6 cloves, or sliced
or chopped coarsely
2 carrots, sliced
1 leek, sliced
1–2 celery sticks, sliced
1 Bouquet Garni
about 2.25 litres/4 pints water

1 Use chopped marrow bones with
a few strips of shin of beef, if
possible. Put in a roasting tin and
cook in a preheated oven at
230°C/450°F/Gas Mark 8 for
30–50 minutes or until browned.

2 Transfer to a large saucepan with
the other ingredients. Bring to
the boil and remove any scum
from the surface with a large
flat spoon.

3 Cover and simmer gently for
3–4 hours. Strain the stock and
leave to cool. Remove any fat
from the surface and chill. If
stored for more than 24 hours the
stock must be boiled every day,
cooled quickly and chilled again.

4 The stock may be frozen for up to
2 months; place in a large plastic
bag and seal, leaving at least
2.5 cm/1 inch of headspace to
allow for expansion.

Chinese Stock

MAKES
2.5 LITRES/4¹/₂ PINTS

750 g/1 lb 10 oz chicken pieces, trimmed
and chopped
750 g/1 lb 10 oz pork spare ribs
3.75 litres/6 pints cold water
3–4 pieces of fresh root ginger, chopped
3–4 spring onions, each tied into a knot
3–4 tbsp Chinese rice wine or dry sherry

1 Place the chicken and pork in a
large saucepan with the water.
Add the ginger and spring onions.

2 Bring to the boil and skim away
any surface scum using a large
flat spoon. Reduce the heat and
simmer, uncovered, for at least
2–3 hours.

3 Strain the stock, discarding the
chicken, pork, ginger and spring
onions. Add the Chinese rice wine
or sherry, return to the boil, then
simmer for 2–3 minutes.

4 Refrigerate the stock when cool. It
will keep for up to 4–5 days.
Alternatively, it can be frozen in
small containers and defrosted
as required.

Cornflour Paste

Mix 1 part cornflour with about
1.5 parts of cold water. Stir until
smooth. The paste can be used to
thicken sauces.

Fresh Bouquet Garni

1 fresh or dried bay leaf
a few fresh parsley sprigs
a few fresh thyme sprigs

Tie the herbs together with a length
of string or cotton.

Dried Bouquet Garni

1 dried bay leaf
good pinch of dried mixed herbs or any
one herb
good pinch of dried parsley
8–10 black peppercorns
2–4 cloves
1 garlic clove, optional

Put all the ingredients in a small
square of muslin and secure with
string or cotton, leaving a long tail so
it can be tied to the handle of the
pan for easy removal.

How to Use This Book

Each recipe contains a wealth of useful information, including a breakdown of nutritional quantities, preparation and cooking times, and level of difficulty. All of this information is explained in detail below.

A full-colour photograph of the finished dish.

The ingredients for each recipe are listed in the order that they are used.

The nutritional information provided for each recipe is per serving or per portion. Optional ingredients, variations or serving suggestions have not been included in the calculations.

The method is clearly explained with step-by-step instructions that are easy to follow.

Cook's tips provide useful information regarding ingredients or cooking techniques.

The content shown in the sample recipe page:

17

SOUPS

This is a really hearty soup, filled with colour, flavour and goodness, which may be adapted to any vegetables that you have at hand.

Mixed Bean Soup

SERVES 4

1 tbsp vegetable oil
1 red onion, halved and sliced
100 g/3½ oz potato, diced
1 carrot, diced
1 leek, sliced
1 fresh green chilli, sliced
3 garlic cloves, crushed
1 tsp ground coriander
1 tsp chilli powder
1 litre/1¾ pints vegetable stock
450 g/1 lb mixed canned beans, such as red kidney, borlotti, black eye or flageolet, drained and rinsed
salt and pepper
2 tbsp chopped fresh coriander, to garnish

1 Heat the oil in a large pan and add the onion, potato, carrot and leek. Cook, stirring occasionally, for 2 minutes until the vegetables are slightly softened.

2 Add the fresh chilli and garlic and cook for 1 further minute.

3 Stir in the ground coriander, chilli powder and the vegetable stock.

4 Bring the soup to the boil, reduce the heat and cook for 20 minutes or until the vegetables are tender.

5 Stir in the beans, season to taste and cook, stirring occasionally, for a further 10 minutes.

6 Ladle the soup into bowls, garnish with chopped coriander and serve.

NUTRITION
Calories 190; Sugars 9 g; Protein 10 g; Carbohydrate 30 g; Fat 4 g; Saturates 0.5 g

very easy
5 mins
40 mins

COOK'S TIP
Serve this soup with slices of warm corn bread or a cheese loaf.

The number of stars represents the difficulty of each recipe, ranging from very easy (1 star) to challenging (4 stars).

This amount of time represents the preparation of ingredients, including cooling, chilling and soaking times.

This represents the cooking time.

Vegetable Soups

Vegetables offer an enormous range of options for making soups. Often the simplest soups to make, they also provide the most versatility. Think of each vegetable as the growing season unfolds and the innumerable ways each can be used in soups – creamy soups, broths, chunky soups, thick and hearty soups. Vegetables provide simple nourishment or dramatic complexity, pure flavours or fascinating amalgamations, lean and healthy alliances or rich, tempting combinations.

Vegetable soups are endlessly variable and eminently enjoyable – and often beautifully coloured, as well. They can provide a light starter to introduce a meal or a hearty and satisfying main course. While most soups are suitable for preparing ahead, vegetable soups are usually quickly cooked and often keep longer than other soups.

This soup, made with fresh tomatoes, tastes of summer, although it can be made at any time of year as long as the tomatoes are ripe.

Fresh Tomato Soup

SERVES 4

1 kg/2 lb 4 oz ripe plum tomatoes, peeled
2 tsp olive oil
1 large sweet onion, such as Vidalia, chopped finely
1 carrot, chopped finely
1 celery stick, chopped finely
2 garlic cloves, chopped finely or crushed
1 tsp fresh marjoram leaves, or ¼ tsp dried marjoram
450 ml/16 fl oz water
4–5 tbsp double cream, plus extra to garnish
2 tbsp chopped fresh basil leaves
salt and pepper

1 Cut the tomatoes in half and scrape the seeds into a sieve set over a bowl to catch the juice. Reserve the juice and discard the seeds. Chop the tomato flesh into large chunks.

2 Heat the olive oil in a large saucepan. Add the onion, carrot and celery and cook over a medium-low heat for 3–4 minutes, stirring occasionally.

3 Add the tomatoes and their juice, with the garlic and marjoram. Cook for 2 minutes. Stir in the water, reduce the heat and simmer, covered, for about 45 minutes or until the vegetables are very soft, stirring occasionally.

4 Allow the soup to cool slightly, then transfer to a blender or food processor and purée until smooth, working in batches if necessary. (If using a food processor, strain off the cooking liquid and reserve. Purée the soup solids with enough cooking liquid to moisten them, then combine with the remaining liquid.)

5 Return the soup to the saucepan and place over a medium-low heat. Add the cream and stir in the basil. Season with salt and pepper and heat through; do not allow to boil.

6 Ladle the soup into warmed bowls and swirl a little extra cream into each serving. Serve at once.

NUTRITION

Calories 222; Sugars 13 g; Protein 3 g; Carbohydrate 15 g; Fat 17 g; Saturates 9 g

 moderate

10 mins

1 hr

A deep red soup makes a stunning first course – and it's easy in the microwave. A swirl of soured cream gives a very pretty effect.

Beetroot *and* Potato Soup

1 Place the onion, potatoes, apple and water in a large glass or ceramic bowl. Cover and cook in the microwave on High power for 10 minutes.

2 Stir in the cumin seeds and cook on High power for 1 minute.

3 Stir in the beetroot, bay leaf, thyme, lemon juice and stock. Cover and cook on High power for 12 minutes, stirring halfway through. Set aside, uncovered, for 5 minutes.

4 Remove and discard the bay leaf. Strain the vegetables and reserve the liquid in a jug.

5 Place the vegetables with a little of the reserved liquid in a food processor or blender and process to a smooth and creamy purée. Alternatively, either mash the vegetables with a potato masher or press through a sieve.

6 Pour the vegetable purée into a clean bowl with the reserved liquid and mix well. Season with salt and pepper to taste. Cover and cook on High power for 4–5 minutes or until piping hot.

7 Serve the soup in warmed bowls. Swirl 1 tablespoon of soured cream into each serving and garnish with a few sprigs of fresh dill.

SERVES 4

1 onion, chopped
350 g/12 oz potatoes, diced
1 small cooking apple, peeled, cored and grated
3 tbsp water
1 tsp cumin seeds
500 g/1 lb 2 oz cooked beetroot, peeled and diced
1 bay leaf
pinch of dried thyme
1 tsp lemon juice
600 ml/1 pint hot vegetable stock
4 tbsp soured cream
salt and pepper
fresh dill sprigs, to garnish

NUTRITION
Calories *120*; Sugars *11 g*; Protein *4 g*; Carbohydrate *22 g*; Fat *2 g*; Saturates *1 g*

 easy

20 mins

30 mins

The parsnip and carrot bring a balancing sweetness to the aubergines in this delicious soup.

Aubergine Soup

SERVES 4

1 tbsp olive oil, plus extra for brushing
750 g/1 lb 10 oz aubergines, halved lengthways
1 carrot, halved
1 small parsnip, halved
2 onions, chopped finely
3 garlic cloves, chopped finely
1 litre/1¾ pints vegetable stock
¼ tsp fresh thyme leaves, or a pinch of dried thyme
1 bay leaf
⅛ tsp ground coriander
1 tbsp tomato purée
150 ml/5 fl oz single cream
freshly squeezed lemon juice
salt and pepper

lemon-garlic seasoning
grated rind of ½ lemon
1 garlic clove, chopped finely
3 tbsp chopped fresh parsley

NUTRITION
Calories *130*; Sugars *9 g*; Protein *3 g*;
Carbohydrate *12 g*; Fat *8 g*; Saturates *3 g*

moderate
20 mins
1 hr 15 mins

1 Oil a shallow roasting tin and add the aubergines, cut sides down, and the carrot and parsnip. Brush the vegetables with oil. Roast in a preheated oven at 200°C/400°F/Gas Mark 6 for 30 minutes, turning once.

2 When cool enough to handle, scrape the aubergine flesh from the skin, or scoop it out, then roughly chop. Cut the carrot and parsnip into chunks.

3 Heat the oil in a large saucepan over a medium-low heat. Add the onions and garlic and cook for about 5 minutes, stirring frequently, until softened. Add the aubergine, parsnip, carrot, stock, thyme, bay leaf, coriander and tomato purée, with a little salt. Stir to combine. Cover and simmer for 30 minutes or until tender.

4 Allow the soup to cool slightly, then transfer to a blender or food processor and purée until smooth, working in batches if necessary. (If using a food processor, strain off the cooking liquid and reserve. Purée the soup solids with enough cooking liquid to moisten them, then combine with the remaining liquid.)

5 Return the puréed soup to the saucepan and stir in the cream. Reheat the soup over a low heat for about 10 minutes or until hot. Adjust the seasoning, adding lemon juice to taste.

6 To make the lemon-garlic seasoning, chop together the lemon rind, garlic and parsley until very fine and well mixed. Ladle the soup into warm bowls, then garnish with the lemon-garlic seasoning.

For the most robust flavour, use bacon that has been fairly heavily smoked and has a pronounced taste; for a more delicate soup, use unsmoked bacon.

Smoky Green Bean Soup

1 Heat the oil in a large wide saucepan over a medium heat. Add the bacon and cook for 8–10 minutes or until golden. Remove the bacon from the pan with a slotted spoon and drain on paper towels. Pour off all the fat from the pan.

2 Add the onion and garlic to the pan and cook for about 3 minutes, stirring frequently, until the onion begins to soften.

3 Stir in the flour and continue cooking for 2 minutes. Add half of the water and stir well, scraping the bottom of the pan to mix in the flour.

4 Add the leek, carrot, potato, beans and bay leaf. Stir in the remaining water and season with salt and pepper. Bring just to the boil, stirring occasionally, reduce the heat and simmer, partially covered, for 35–40 minutes or until the beans are very tender.

5 Allow the soup to cool slightly, then transfer to a blender or food processor and purée until smooth, working in batches if necessary. (If using a food processor, strain off the cooking liquid and reserve. Purée the soup solids with enough cooking liquid to moisten them, then combine with the remaining liquid.)

6 Return the soup to the saucepan, add the bacon and simmer over a low heat for a few minutes until heated through, stirring occasionally. Taste and adjust the seasoning, adding nutmeg, pepper and, if needed, more salt. Garnish with croûtons.

SERVES 4

1 tbsp oil
100 g/3½ oz lean smoked back bacon, chopped finely
1 onion, chopped finely
1–2 garlic cloves, crushed or chopped finely
2 tbsp plain flour
1.2 litres/2 pints water
1 leek, sliced thinly
1 carrot, chopped finely
1 small potato, chopped finely
500 g/1 lb 2 oz green beans
1 bay leaf
freshly grated nutmeg
salt and pepper
garlic croûtons, to garnish (see page 89)

NUTRITION
Calories *192*; Sugars *7 g*; Protein *9 g*; Carbohydrate *22 g*; Fat *8 g*; Saturates *2 g*

★★★   moderate

    15 mins

    1 hr

This fresh-tasting soup with green beans, cucumber and watercress can be served warm, or chilled on a hot summer day.

Green Soup

SERVES 4

1 tbsp olive oil
1 onion, chopped
1 garlic clove, chopped
200 g/7 oz potato, cut into
  2.5 cm/1 inch cubes
700 ml/1¼ pints vegetable or chicken stock
1 small cucumber or ½ large cucumber, cut
  into chunks
85 g/3 oz watercress
125 g/4½ oz green beans, trimmed and
  halved lengthways
salt and pepper

1 Heat the oil in a large pan and cook the onion and garlic over a medium heat for 3–4 minutes or until softened.

2 Add the cubed potato and cook for a further 2–3 minutes. Stir in the stock and bring to the boil. Reduce the heat and simmer for 5 minutes.

3 Add the cucumber to the pan and cook for a further 3 minutes or until the potatoes are tender. Test by inserting the tip of a knife into the potato cubes – it should pass through easily.

4 Add the watercress and cook until just wilted. Remove from the heat and set aside to cool slightly, then transfer to a food processor and process to a smooth purée. Alternatively, before adding the watercress, mash the vegetables with a potato masher and push through a sieve, then chop the watercress finely and stir into the soup.

5 Bring a small pan of water to the boil and steam the beans for 3–4 minutes or until tender. Add the beans to the soup, season to taste with salt and pepper and warm through. Ladle into warmed soup bowls and serve immediately or set aside to cool and then chill.

NUTRITION
Calories *121*; Sugars *2 g*; Protein *2 g*;
Carbohydrate *10 g*; Fat *8 g*; Saturates *1 g*

 easy

 15–45 mins

 25 mins

🍳 **COOK'S TIP**

Try using 125 g/4½ oz mangetout instead of the beans.

Adding soft cheese to this soup just before serving makes it very special, while the rice and croûtons provide an excellent contrast of textures.

Broccoli Soup

1 Divide the broccoli into small florets and cut off the stems. Peel the large stem, then chop all the stems into small pieces.

2 Heat the butter and oil in a large saucepan over a medium heat and add the onion, leek and carrot. Cook for 3–4 minutes, stirring frequently, until the onion is soft.

3 Add the broccoli stems, rice, water, bay leaf and a pinch of salt. Bring just to the boil and reduce the heat to low. Cover the pan and simmer the soup for 15 minutes. Add the broccoli florets and continue cooking, covered, for 15–20 minutes or until the rice and vegetables are tender. Remove the bay leaf.

4 Season the soup with nutmeg, pepper and, if needed, more salt. Stir in the cream and cream cheese. Simmer over a low heat for a few minutes until heated through, stirring occasionally. Taste, and adjust the seasoning if necessary. Ladle the soup into warmed bowls and garnish with croûtons.

SERVES 4

400 g/14 oz broccoli (from 1 large head)
10 g/⅓ oz butter
1 tsp oil
1 onion, chopped finely
1 leek, sliced thinly
1 small carrot, chopped finely
3 tbsp white rice
850 ml/1½ pints water
1 bay leaf
freshly grated nutmeg
4 tbsp double cream
100 g/3½ oz cream cheese
salt and pepper
croûtons, to garnish (see Cook's Tip)

NUTRITION
Calories *208*; Sugars *5 g*; Protein *6 g*;
Carbohydrate *10 g*; Fat *16 g*; Saturates *9 g*

⭐⭐⭐ moderate
🕐 15 mins
🕑 40 mins

 COOK'S TIP

To make croûtons, remove the crusts from thick slices of white bread, then cut the bread into dice. Fry in vegetable oil, stirring constantly, until evenly browned, then drain on kitchen paper.

This soup has a rich, brilliant colour and an intense, pure flavour. Ready-washed spinach makes it especially quick to make.

Spinach Soup

SERVES 4

1 tbsp olive oil
1 onion, halved and sliced thinly
1 leek, split lengthways and sliced thinly
1 potato, finely diced
1 litre/1¾ pints water
2 fresh marjoram sprigs or ¼ tsp dried marjoram
2 fresh thyme sprigs or ¼ tsp dried thyme
1 bay leaf
400 g/14 oz young spinach
freshly grated nutmeg
salt and pepper
4 tbsp single cream, to serve

1 Heat the oil in a heavy-based pan over a medium heat. Add the onion and leek and cook, stirring occasionally, for about 3 minutes or until they are just beginning to soften.

2 Add the potato, water, marjoram, thyme and bay leaf and season with a pinch of salt. Bring to the boil, reduce the heat, cover and cook gently for about 25 minutes or until the vegetables are tender. Remove the bay leaf and the herb stems.

3 Add the spinach and continue cooking for 3–4 minutes, stirring frequently, until it is completely wilted. Remove the pan from the heat and set aside to cool slightly.

4 Transfer the soup to a blender or food processor and process to a smooth purée, working in batches if necessary. (If using a food processor, strain off the cooking liquid and reserve. Process the soup solids with enough cooking liquid to moisten them, then combine with the remaining liquid.)

5 Return the soup to the pan and thin with a little more water, if wished. Season to taste with salt, pepper and nutmeg. Place over a low heat and simmer until reheated. Ladle the soup into warmed bowls and swirl a tablespoonful of cream into each serving.

NUTRITION
Calories 98; Sugars 4 g; Protein 4 g; Carbohydrate 12 g; Fat 4 g; Saturates 1 g

 easy

10 mins

40 mins

The exotic flavours give this simple soup a lift. If you wish, use bought ginger purée instead of grating it; add to taste, as the strength varies.

Parsnip Soup *with* Ginger

1 Heat the olive oil in a large pan over a medium heat. Add the onion and leek and cook, stirring occasionally, for about 5 minutes or until softened.

2 Add the parsnips, carrots, ginger, garlic, grated orange rind, water and a pinch of salt. Reduce the heat, cover and simmer, stirring occasionally, for about 40 minutes or until the vegetables are soft.

3 Remove from the heat and set aside to cool slightly, then transfer to a blender or food processor and process to a smooth purée, in batches if necessary.

4 Return the soup to the pan and stir in the orange juice. Add a little water or more orange juice, if you prefer a thinner consistency. Taste and adjust the seasoning with salt and pepper.

5 Simmer for about 10 minutes to heat through. Ladle into warmed bowls, garnish with chives or slivers of spring onion and serve immediately.

SERVES 4

2 tsp olive oil
1 large onion, chopped
1 large leek, sliced
800 g/1 lb 12 oz parsnips, sliced
2 carrots, sliced thinly
4 tbsp grated fresh root ginger
2–3 garlic cloves, chopped finely
grated rind of ½ orange
1.4 litres/2½ pints water
225 ml/8 fl oz orange juice
salt and pepper
snipped chives or slivers of spring onion,
   to garnish

NUTRITION
Calories *151*; Sugars *19 g*; Protein *4 g*;
Carbohydrate *29 g*; Fat *3 g*; Saturates *0 g*

⭐⭐   easy
            10 mins
            55 mins

 COOK'S TIP

You could make the soup using equal amounts (450 g/1 lb each) of carrots and parsnips.

This soup has an intense, earthy flavour that brings to mind woodland aromas. It makes a memorable, rich-tasting starter.

Wild Mushroom Soup

SERVES 4

25 g/1 oz dried porcini mushrooms
350 ml/12 fl oz boiling water
125 g/4½ oz fresh porcini mushrooms
2 tsp olive oil
1 celery stick, chopped
1 carrot, chopped
1 onion, chopped
3 garlic cloves, crushed
1.2 litres/2 pints vegetable stock or water
leaves from 2 fresh thyme sprigs
15 g/½ oz butter
3 tbsp dry or medium sherry
2–3 tbsp soured cream
salt and pepper
chopped fresh parsley, to garnish

NUTRITION
Calories *130*; Sugars *5 g*; Protein *3 g*;
Carbohydrate *6 g*; Fat *9 g*; Saturates *5 g*

moderate

20 mins

1 hr

1 Soak the dried mushrooms in a bowl with the boiling water, for 10–15 minutes.

2 Brush or wash the fresh mushrooms. Trim and reserve the stems. Slice any large mushroom caps.

3 Heat the oil in a large saucepan over a medium heat. Add the celery, carrot, onion and mushroom stems. Cook, stirring frequently, for about 8 minutes or until the onion begins to colour. Stir in the garlic and cook for 1 minute.

4 Add the vegetable stock or water and thyme with a pinch of salt. Add the soaked dried mushrooms. Strain the soaking liquid through a muslin-lined strainer into the pan. Bring to the boil, reduce the heat, partially cover and simmer gently for 30–40 minutes or until the carrots are tender.

5 Remove the pan from the heat and set aside to cool slightly, then transfer the soup solids with enough of the cooking liquid to moisten to a blender or food processor and purée until smooth. Return it to the pan, combine with the remaining cooking liquid, cover and simmer gently.

6 Meanwhile, melt the butter in a frying pan over a medium heat. Add the fresh mushroom caps and season to taste with salt and pepper. Cook, stirring occasionally, for about 8 minutes or until they start to colour. When the pan becomes dry, add the sherry and cook briefly.

7 Add the mushrooms and sherry to the soup. Taste and adjust the seasoning, if necessary. Ladle into warmed soup bowls, put a spoonful of soured cream in each and garnish with parsley.

Include some pungent greens in this soup, if you can. They add a wonderful gutsy flavour and, of course, are very good for you!

Beans *and* Greens Soup

1 Cover the beans with cold water and soak for 6 hours or overnight. Drain, put in a pan and add water to cover by 5 cm/2 inches. Bring to the boil and boil for 10 minutes. Drain and rinse.

2 Heat the olive oil in a large pan over a medium heat. Add the onions and cook, stirring occasionally, for about 3–4 minutes or until just softened. Add the garlic, celery and carrots and continue cooking for 2 minutes.

3 Add the water, beans, thyme, marjoram and bay leaf. When the mixture begins to simmer, reduce the heat to low. Cover and simmer gently, stirring occasionally, for about 1¼ hours or until the beans are tender. The cooking time will vary depending on the type of bean. Season to taste with salt and pepper.

4 Remove the pan from the heat and set aside to cool slightly, then transfer 450 ml/16 fl oz to a blender or food processor. Process to a smooth purée and recombine with the soup.

5 Cut the greens crossways into thin ribbons, keeping tender leaves, such as spinach, separate. Add the thicker leaves and cook gently for 10 minutes. Stir in any remaining greens and cook for a further 5–10 minutes or until all the greens are tender. Taste and adjust the seasoning if necessary. Ladle the soup into warmed bowls and serve immediately.

SERVES 4

250 g/9 oz dried haricot or cannellini beans
1 tbsp olive oil
2 onions, chopped finely
4 garlic cloves, chopped finely
1 celery stick, sliced thinly
2 carrots, halved and sliced thinly
1.2 litres/2 pints water
¼ tsp dried thyme
¼ tsp dried marjoram
1 bay leaf
115 g/4 oz leafy greens, such as chard, mustard, spinach and kale, washed
salt and pepper

NUTRITION
Calories *282*; Sugars *8 g*; Protein *16 g*; Carbohydrate *46 g*; Fat *4 g*; Saturates *1 g*

⭐⭐   easy

🌫   6 hrs 15 mins

🕐   2 hrs

This soup is surprisingly delicate. The yellow peas give it an appealing light colour, while the parsnips add an aromatic flavour.

Split Pea *and* Parsnip Soup

SERVES 4

250 g/9 oz split yellow peas
1 tbsp olive oil
1 onion, chopped finely
1 small leek, chopped finely
3 garlic cloves, chopped finely
2 parsnips, sliced (about 225 g/8 oz)
2 litres/3½ pints water
10 fresh sage leaves or ¼ tsp dried sage
pinch of dried thyme
¼ tsp ground coriander
1 bay leaf
salt and pepper
freshly grated nutmeg
chopped fresh coriander leaves or parsley, to garnish

NUTRITION
Calories *270*; Sugars *5 g*; Protein *16 g*;
Carbohydrate *39 g*; Fat *7 g*; Saturates *1 g*

 easy

10 mins

1 hr

1 Rinse the peas well under cold running water. Put in a pan and cover generously with water. Bring to the boil and boil for 3 minutes, skimming off the foam from the surface. Drain the peas.

2 Heat the oil in a large pan over a medium heat. Add the onion and leek and cook, stirring occasionally, for about 3 minutes or until just softened. Add the garlic and parsnips and continue cooking, stirring occasionally, for 2 minutes.

3 Add the peas, water, sage, thyme, ground coriander and bay leaf. Bring almost to the boil, reduce the heat, cover and simmer gently for about 40 minutes or until the vegetables are very soft. Remove the bay leaf.

4 Remove the pan from the heat and set aside to cool slightly, then transfer the mixture to a blender or food processor and process to a smooth purée, in batches if necessary. (If using a food processor, strain off the cooking liquid and reserve. Purée the soup solids with enough cooking liquid to moisten them, then combine with the remaining liquid.)

5 Return the soup to the pan and thin with a little more water, if wished. Season generously with salt, pepper and nutmeg. Place over a low heat and simmer until reheated. Ladle into warmed soup plates and garnish with fresh coriander leaves or parsley.

This is a hearty and flavourful soup that is good on its own or spooned over cooked rice or baked potatoes for a more substantial meal.

Vegetable Chilli

1 Brush the aubergine slices on one side with olive oil. Heat half the oil in a large, heavy-based frying pan over a medium-high heat. Add the aubergine slices, oiled side up, and cook for 5–6 minutes or until browned on that side. Turn the slices over, cook on the other side until browned and transfer to a plate. Cut into bite-sized pieces.

2 Heat the remaining oil in a large saucepan over a medium heat. Add the onion and peppers and cook, stirring occasionally, for 3–4 minutes or until the onion is just softened, but not browned. Add the garlic and continue cooking for 2–3 minutes or until the onion us just beginning to colour.

3 Add the tomatoes, chilli powder, cumin and oregano. Season to taste with salt and pepper. Bring just to the boil, reduce the heat, cover and simmer gently for 15 minutes.

4 Add the sliced courgettes, aubergine pieces and kidney beans. Stir in the water and the tomato purée. Bring back to the boil, then cover the pan and continue simmering for about 45 minutes or until the vegetables are tender. Taste and adjust the seasoning if necessary. If you prefer a hotter dish, stir in a little more chilli powder.

5 Ladle into warmed bowls and top with spring onions and cheese.

SERVES 4

1 medium aubergine, peeled if wished, cut into 2.5 cm/1 inch slices
1 tbsp olive oil, plus extra for brushing
1 large red or yellow onion, chopped finely
2 red or yellow peppers, deseeded and chopped finely
3–4 garlic cloves, chopped finely or crushed
800 g/28 oz canned chopped tomatoes
1 tbsp mild chilli powder
½ tsp ground cumin
½ tsp dried oregano
2 small courgettes, quartered lengthways and sliced
400 g/14 oz canned kidney beans, drained and rinsed
450 ml/16 fl oz water
1 tbsp tomato purée
6 spring onions, chopped finely
115 g/4 oz grated Cheddar cheese
salt and pepper

NUTRITION
Calories 213; Sugars 11 g; Protein 12 g; Carbohydrate 21 g; Fat 10 g; Saturates 5 g

 easy

 10 mins

1 hr 15 mins

This soup is simple and satisfying, with subtle flavours. It uses ingredients you are likely to have on hand, so it's ideal for a last-minute meal.

Tomato *and* Lentil Soup

SERVES 6

1 tbsp olive oil
1 leek, sliced thinly
1 large carrot, quartered and sliced thinly
1 large onion, chopped finely
2 garlic cloves, chopped finely
250 g/9 oz split red lentils
1.2 litres/2 pints water
350 ml/12 fl oz tomato juice
400 g/14 oz canned chopped tomatoes
¼ tsp ground cumin
¼ tsp ground coriander
1 bay leaf
salt and pepper
chopped fresh dill or parsley, to garnish

NUTRITION
Calories *194*; Sugars *9 g*; Protein *12 g*;
Carbohydrate *33 g*; Fat *3 g*; Saturates *0 g*

easy

10 mins

1 hr

1 Heat the oil in a large pan over a medium heat. Add the leek, carrot, onion and garlic. Cover and cook, stirring occasionally, for 4–5 minutes or until the vegetables are slightly softened.

2 Rinse and drain the lentils (check for any small stones). Add the lentils to the pan and stir in the water, tomato juice and tomatoes. Add the cumin, coriander and bay leaf with a pinch of salt. Bring to the boil, reduce the heat and simmer gently for about 45 minutes or until the vegetables are tender. Remove the bay leaf.

3 Remove the pan from the heat and set aside to cool slightly. If you prefer a smooth soup, transfer the mixture to a blender or food processor and process to a smooth purée, working in batches if necessary. (If using a food processor, strain off the cooking liquid and reserve. Purée the soup solids with enough cooking liquid to moisten them, then combine with the remaining liquid.) Process only about half of the mixture if you prefer a soup with a chunkier texture.

4 Return the puréed soup to the pan and stir to blend. Season with salt and pepper to taste. Simmer over a medium-low heat until reheated.

5 Ladle the soup into warmed bowls, garnish with dill or parsley and serve.

This soup is a typical Indian treatment of lentils, called dhal. Often dhals are served as a thick purée, but in this version the consistency is slightly thinner to make it easier for spooning.

Curried Lentil Soup *with* Fried Onions

1 Heat the olive oil in a large saucepan over a medium heat. Add the onion and cook for 4–5 minutes, stirring frequently, until it just begins to brown. Add the leek, carrot and garlic and cook for 2 minutes, stirring occasionally.

2 Stir in the chilli purée, ginger, garam masala or curry powder, cumin and turmeric. Add the water and stir to mix well.

3 Rinse and drain the lentils or split peas (check for any small stones). Add to the saucepan. Bring to the boil, reduce the heat, cover and simmer gently for 35 minutes or until the lentils and vegetables are very soft, stirring occasionally.

4 Allow the soup to cool slightly, then transfer to a blender or food processor and purée until smooth, working in batches if necessary. (If using a food processor, strain off the cooking liquid and reserve. Purée the soup solids with enough cooking liquid to moisten them, then combine with the remaining liquid.)

5 Return the soup to the saucepan and simmer over a low heat. Season with salt and pepper to taste.

6 For the fried onions, heat about 1 cm/½ inch oil in a small frying pan over a medium-high heat until it begins to smoke. Drop in about one-third of the onion slices and fry until deep golden brown. Using a slotted spoon, transfer to paper towels and drain. Cook the remainder of the onion slices in batches.

7 Ladle the soup into warmed bowls and scatter the fried onions over the top. Serve the soup immediately.

SERVES 4

2 tsp olive oil
1 large onion, chopped finely
1 large leek, sliced thinly
1 large carrot, grated
1–2 garlic cloves, chopped finely
½ tsp chilli purée
½ tsp grated peeled fresh root ginger or ginger purée
½ tsp garam masala or curry powder
¼ tsp ground cumin
⅛ tsp ground turmeric
1.2 litres/2 pints water
250 g/9 oz split red lentils or yellow split peas
salt and pepper

to garnish
1 red onion, halved and sliced thinly into half-rings
oil, for frying

NUTRITION
Calories *232*; Sugars *6 g*; Protein *11 g*; Carbohydrate *31 g*; Fat *8 g*; Saturates *1 g*

 moderate
 10 mins
10 mins

55 mins

In this simple-to-make soup, the flavours meld after blending to create a delicious taste. It is also very healthy and looks appealing.

Golden Vegetable Soup

SERVES 6

1 tbsp olive oil
1 onion, chopped finely
1 garlic clove, chopped finely
1 carrot, halved and sliced thinly
450 g/1 lb green cabbage, shredded
400 g/14 oz canned chopped tomatoes
½ tsp dried thyme
2 bay leaves
1.5 litres/2¾ pints vegetable stock
200 g/7 oz Puy lentils
450 ml/16 fl oz water
salt and pepper
fresh coriander leaves or parsley, to garnish

1 Heat the oil in a large pan over a medium heat. Add the onion, garlic and carrot and cook, stirring occasionally, for 3–4 minutes. Add the cabbage and cook for a further 2 minutes.

2 Add the tomatoes, thyme and 1 bay leaf, then pour in the stock. Bring to the boil, reduce the heat, partially cover and simmer for about 45 minutes or until the vegetables are tender.

3 Meanwhile, put the lentils in another pan with the remaining bay leaf and the water. Bring just to the boil, reduce the heat and simmer for about 25 minutes or until tender. Drain off any remaining water and set aside.

4 Remove the soup from the heat and set aside to cool slightly, then transfer to a blender or food processor and process to a smooth purée, working in batches, if necessary. (If using a food processor, strain off the cooking liquid and reserve. Purée the soup solids with enough cooking liquid to moisten them, then combine with the remaining liquid.)

5 Return the soup to the pan and add the cooked lentils. Taste and adjust the seasoning, if necessary, and cook for about 10 minutes to heat through. Ladle into warmed bowls and garnish with coriander leaves or parsley.

NUTRITION
Calories *155*; Sugars *5 g*; Protein *10 g*;
Carbohydrate *22 g*; Fat *3 g*; Saturates *0 g*

  easy

  10 mins

  1 hr 30 mins

This rustic vegetable soup is appealing in its simplicity. Served with ciabatta, focaccia or garlic bread, it makes a good light lunch.

Fennel *and* Broccoli Soup

1 Rinse the barley and drain. Bring 450 ml/16 fl oz of the stock to the boil in a small pan. Add the bay leaf, thyme and a pinch of salt. Stir in the barley, reduce the heat, partially cover and simmer for 30–40 minutes or until tender.

2 Cut the broccoli into florets and peel the stems. Cut the stems into very thin batons, about 2.5 cm/1 inch long. Cut the florets into small slivers and reserve them separately.

3 Heat the oil in a large pan over a medium-low heat and add the leek and garlic. Cook, stirring frequently, for about 5 minutes or until softened. Add the celery, fennel and broccoli stems and cook for 2 minutes.

4 Stir in the remaining stock and bring to the boil. Add the barley with its cooking liquid. Season to taste with salt and pepper. Reduce the heat, cover the pan and simmer gently, stirring occasionally, for 10 minutes.

5 Uncover the pan and adjust the heat so the soup bubbles gently. Stir in the broccoli florets and cook for a further 10–12 minutes or until the broccoli is tender. Stir in the basil. Taste and adjust the seasoning if necessary. Ladle into warmed bowls and serve with plenty of Parmesan cheese to sprinkle over.

SERVES 4

55 g/2 oz pearl barley
1.5 litres/2¾ pints chicken or vegetable stock
1 bay leaf
½ tsp chopped fresh thyme leaves, or ⅛ tsp dried thyme
250 g/9 oz broccoli
2 tsp olive oil
1 large leek, halved lengthways and chopped finely
2 garlic cloves, chopped finely
1 celery stick, sliced thinly
1 large fennel bulb, sliced thinly
1 tbsp chopped fresh basil
salt and pepper
freshly grated Parmesan cheese, to serve

NUTRITION
Calories *108*; Sugars *3 g*; Protein *6 g*; Carbohydrate *15 g*; Fat *3 g*; Saturates *0 g*

 moderate

15 mins

1 hr 15 mins

Although it is generally classed as a grain, wild rice is actually a native North American grass that grows in water. It adds a delicious texture to this soup.

Wild Rice *and* Spinach Soup

SERVES 4

2 tsp olive oil

85 g/3 oz smoked back bacon, chopped finely

1 large onion, chopped finely

125 g/4½ oz wild rice, rinsed in cold water and drained

1.2 litres/2 pints water

1–2 garlic cloves, chopped or crushed finely

1 bay leaf

70 g/2½ oz plain flour

450 ml/16 fl oz milk

225 g/8 oz spinach leaves, chopped finely

225 ml/8 fl oz double cream

freshly grated nutmeg

salt and pepper

croûtons, to garnish

NUTRITION

Calories *602*; Sugars *12 g*; Protein *14 g*; Carbohydrate *51 g*; Fat *39 g*; Saturates *20 g*

  easy

15 mins

 1 hr 15 mins

1 Heat the oil in a large saucepan over a medium heat. Add the bacon and cook for 6–7 minutes or until lightly browned. Add the onion and wild rice and continue cooking for 3–4 minutes, stirring frequently, until the onion softens.

2 Add the water, garlic and bay leaf and season with a little salt and pepper. Bring to the boil, reduce the heat, cover and simmer very gently for about 1 hour or until some of the grains of wild rice have split open.

3 Put the flour in a mixing bowl and very slowly whisk in enough of the milk to make a thick paste. Add the remainder of the milk, whisking to make a smooth liquid. Put the flour and milk mixture in a saucepan and ladle in as much of the rice cooking liquid as possible. Bring to the boil, stirring almost constantly. Reduce the heat so that the liquid just bubbles gently and cook for 10 minutes, stirring occasionally. Add the chopped spinach and cook for 1–2 minutes or until wilted.

4 Allow the soup to cool slightly, then transfer to a blender or food processor and purée, working in batches if necessary. (If using a food processor, strain off the cooking liquid and reserve. Purée the soup solids with enough cooking liquid to moisten them, then combine with the remaining liquid.)

5 Combine the puréed soup with the rice mixture in a saucepan and place over a medium-low heat. Stir in the cream and a grating of nutmeg. Simmer the soup until reheated. Taste and adjust the seasoning, if needed, ladle into warmed bowls and garnish with croûtons.

This healthy and colourful soup makes good use of your herb garden. The fresh herbs give it a vibrant flavour.

Vegetable Soup *with* Bulgur

1 Heat the oil in a large pan over a medium-low heat and add the onions and garlic. Cook for 5–8 minutes, stirring occasionally, until the onions soften.

2 Stir in the bulgur wheat and continue cooking, stirring constantly, for 1 minute.

3 Layer the tomatoes, pumpkin and courgette in the pan.

4 Combine half the water with the tomato purée, chilli purée and a pinch of salt. Pour over the vegetables. Cover and simmer for 15 minutes.

5 Uncover the pan and stir. Put all the herbs and the rocket on top of the soup and layer the peas over them. Pour in the remaining water and gradually bring to the boil. Reduce the heat and simmer for about 20–25 minutes or until all the vegetables are tender.

6 Stir the soup. Taste and adjust the seasoning, adding salt and pepper, if necessary, and a little more chilli purée if you wish. Ladle into warmed bowls and serve with Parmesan cheese.

SERVES 4

1 tbsp olive oil
2 onions, chopped
3 garlic cloves, chopped finely or crushed
55 g/2 oz bulgur wheat
5 tomatoes, peeled and sliced or 400 g/14 oz canned plum tomatoes in juice
225 g/8 oz peeled pumpkin, diced
1 large courgette, quartered lengthways and sliced
1 litre/1¾ pints boiling water
2 tbsp tomato purée
¼ tsp chilli purée
40 g/1½ oz chopped mixed fresh oregano, basil and flat leaf parsley
25 g/1 oz rocket leaves, chopped coarsely
175 g/6 oz shelled fresh or frozen peas
salt and pepper
freshly grated Parmesan cheese, to serve

NUTRITION
Calories *93*; Sugars *8 g*; Protein *5 g*; Carbohydrate *13 g*; Fat *3 g*; Saturates *0 g*

    easy

    10 mins

    1 hr

Hot *and* Spicy

Soups are a part of nearly every meal in the Far East, and are usually served between courses to clear the palate. This chapter provides a range of soups from all over the Far East, from thick Indian dhal soups to hot, sour Chinese vegetarian soups and combinations of seafood and noodles. All the ingredients are readily available from good stores, and although several recipes demand a little time, all are worth any extra effort in the making.

SOUPS

Parsnips make a delicious soup as they have a slightly sweet flavour. In this recipe, spices are added to complement this sweetness.

Curried Parsnip Soup

SERVES 4

1 tbsp vegetable oil
15 g/½ oz butter
1 red onion, chopped
3 parsnips, chopped
2 garlic cloves, crushed
2 tsp garam masala
½ tsp chilli powder
1 tbsp plain flour
850 ml/1½ pints vegetable stock
grated rind and juice of 1 lemon
salt and pepper
lemon rind, cut into long strips, to garnish

1 Heat the oil and butter in a large saucepan until the butter has melted. Add the onion, parsnips and garlic and sauté, stirring frequently, for about 5–7 minutes or until the vegetables have softened, but not coloured.

2 Add the garam masala and chilli powder and cook, stirring constantly, for 30 seconds. Sprinkle in the flour, mixing well and cook, stirring constantly, for a further 30 seconds.

3 Stir in the stock, lemon rind and juice and bring to the boil. Reduce the heat and simmer for 20 minutes.

4 Remove some of the vegetable pieces with a slotted spoon and reserve until required. Transfer the remaining soup and vegetables to a blender or food processor and process for about 1 minute or until a smooth purée is formed. Alternatively, press the vegetables through a sieve with the back of a wooden spoon.

5 Return the soup to a clean saucepan and stir in the reserved vegetables. Heat the soup through for 2 minutes or until piping hot.

6 Season to taste with salt and pepper, then transfer to soup bowls, garnish with lemon rind strips and serve.

NUTRITION

Calories *152*; Sugars *7 g*; Protein *3 g*;
Carbohydrate *18 g*; Fat *8 g*; Saturates *3 g*

 very easy

10 mins

35 mins

This soup can be frozen, so it is a good way to use up a glut of courgettes from the garden. Adding curry powder gives the flavour a lift.

Curried Courgette Soup

1 Melt the butter in a large saucepan over a medium heat. Add the onion and cook for about 3 minutes or until it begins to soften.

2 Add the courgettes, stock and curry powder, with a large pinch of salt if using unsalted stock. Bring the soup to the boil, reduce the heat, cover and cook gently for about 25 minutes or until the vegetables are tender.

3 Allow the soup to cool slightly, then transfer it to a blender or food processor, working in batches if necessary. Purée the soup until just smooth, but still with green flecks. (If using a food processor, strain off the cooking liquid and reserve. Purée the soup solids with enough cooking liquid to moisten them, then combine with the remaining liquid.)

4 Return the soup to the saucepan and stir in the soured cream. Reheat gently over a low heat just until hot, but be careful not to allow the soup to boil.

5 Taste and adjust the seasoning, if needed. Ladle the soup into warmed bowls and serve, garnished with a swirl of soured cream and croûtons.

SERVES 4

10 g/⅓ oz butter
1 large onion, chopped finely
900 g/2 lb courgettes, sliced
450 ml/16 fl oz vegetable stock
1 tsp curry powder
salt and pepper
125 ml/4 fl oz soured cream

to garnish
4 tbsp soured cream
croûtons (see page 25)

NUTRITION
Calories *147*; Sugars *8 g*; Protein *6 g*;
Carbohydrate *10 g*; Fat *9 g*; Saturates *5 g*

⊛⊛ easy

◔ 10 mins

◑ 35 mins

🎩 COOK'S TIP

Stock made from a cube or liquid stock base is fine for this soup. In this case, you may wish to add a little more soured cream. The soup freezes well, but freeze it without the cream and add before serving.

Dhal is a delicious Indian lentil dish. This soup is a variation on the theme – it is made with red lentils and spiced with curry powder.

Curried Lentil Soup

SERVES 4

25 g/1 oz butter
2 garlic cloves, crushed
1 onion, chopped
½ tsp turmeric
1 tsp garam masala
¼ tsp chilli powder
1 tsp ground cumin
1 kg/2 lb 4 oz canned chopped tomatoes, drained
175 g/6 oz red lentils
2 tsp lemon juice
600 ml/1 pint vegetable stock
300 ml/10 fl oz coconut milk
salt and pepper
chopped coriander and lemon slices, to garnish
naan bread, to serve

1 Melt the butter in a large saucepan and sauté the crushed garlic and onion for 2–3 minutes, stirring. Add the turmeric, garam masala, chilli powder and ground cumin and cook for a further 30 seconds.

2 Stir in the tomatoes, red lentils, lemon juice, vegetable stock and coconut milk and bring to the boil.

3 Reduce the heat and simmer for 25–30 minutes or until the lentils are tender and cooked.

4 Season to taste and spoon the soup into a warm tureen. Garnish with the chopped coriander and lemon slices and serve with warm naan bread.

NUTRITION
Calories 284; Sugars 13 g; Protein 16 g; Carbohydrate 38 g; Fat 9 g; Saturates 5 g

easy

5 mins

40 mins

🎩 **COOK'S TIP**

You can buy cans of coconut milk from supermarkets and delicatessens. It can also be made by grating creamed coconut, which comes in the form of a solid bar, and mixing it with water.

Avocado has a rich flavour and colour which makes a creamy flavoured soup. It is best served chilled, but may be eaten warm as well.

Avocado *and* Vegetable Soup

1 Peel the avocado and mash the flesh with a fork, stir in the lemon juice and reserve until required.

2 Heat the vegetable oil in a large saucepan. Add the sweetcorn, tomatoes, garlic, leek and chilli and sauté over a low heat for 2–3 minutes or until the vegetables have softened.

3 Put half the vegetable mixture in a blender or food processor, together with the mashed avocado, and process until smooth. Transfer the mixture to a clean saucepan.

4 Add the vegetable stock, milk and reserved vegetables and cook over a low heat for 3–4 minutes or until hot. Transfer to warmed individual serving bowls, garnish with shredded leek and serve immediately.

SERVES 4

1 large, ripe avocado
2 tbsp lemon juice
1 tbsp vegetable oil
50 g/1¾ oz canned sweetcorn, drained
2 tomatoes, peeled and deseeded
1 garlic clove, crushed
1 leek, chopped
1 red chilli, chopped
425 ml/¾ pint vegetable stock
150 ml/5 fl oz milk
shredded leek, to garnish

NUTRITION
Calories *167*; Sugars *5 g*; Protein *4 g*;
Carbohydrate *8 g*; Fat *13 g*; Saturates *3 g*

⭐ very easy

🕐 15 mins

🕐 10 mins

🍳 **COOK'S TIP**

If serving chilled, transfer from the food processor to a bowl, stir in the vegetable stock and milk, cover and chill in the refrigerator for at least 4 hours.

This is a very colourful and delicious soup. If spinach is not in season, watercress or lettuce can be used instead.

Spinach *and* Tofu Soup

SERVES 4

1 cake of firm tofu
125 g/4½ oz spinach leaves without stems
700 ml/1¼ pints water or fresh vegetable stock
1 tbsp light soy sauce
salt and pepper

1 Using a sharp knife to avoid squashing it, cut the tofu into small pieces about 5 mm/¼ inch thick.

2 Wash the spinach leaves under cold, running water and drain well.

3 Cut the spinach leaves into small pieces or shreds, discarding any discoloured leaves and tough stalks. (If possible, use fresh young spinach leaves, which have not yet developed tough ribs. Otherwise, it is important to cut out all the ribs and stems for this soup.) Set the spinach aside.

4 In a preheated wok or large frying pan, bring the water or vegetable stock to a rolling boil. Add the tofu cubes and light soy sauce, bring back to the boil and simmer for about 2 minutes over a medium heat.

5 Add the spinach and simmer for 1 more minute, stirring gently. Skim the surface of the soup to make it clear and season to taste.

6 Transfer the soup to either a warmed soup tureen or warmed individual serving bowls. If you wish, serve with chopsticks to pick up the spinach and chunks of tofu and a broad, shallow spoon for drinking the soup.

NUTRITION

Calories *33*; Sugars *1 g*; Protein *4 g*; Carbohydrate *1 g*; Fat *2 g*; Saturates *0.2 g*

 very easy

 15 mins

 10 mins

COOK'S TIP

Soup is an integral part of a Chinese meal; it is usually presented in a large bowl in the centre of the table, and consumed as the meal progresses. It serves as a refresher between dishes and as a beverage throughout the meal.

This healthy soup is made with an unusual combination of fruits and vegetables, creating a tantalising flavour that will keep people guessing.

Sweet *and* Sour Cabbage Soup

1 Put the sultanas in a bowl, cover with orange juice and set aside for 15 minutes.

2 Heat the oil in a large pan over a medium heat. Add the onion and cook, stirring occasionally, for 3–4 minutes or until it starts to soften. Add the cabbage and cook for a further 2 minutes, but do not allow it to brown.

3 Add the apples and apple juice, cover and cook for 5 minutes. Stir in the tomatoes, tomato or vegetable juice, pineapple and water. Season to taste with salt and pepper and add the vinegar. Add the sultanas with the orange juice. Bring to the boil, reduce the heat, partially cover and simmer for 1 hour or until the fruit and vegetables are tender.

4 Remove the pan from the heat and set aside to cool slightly. Transfer the soup to a blender or food processor and process to a smooth purée, working in batches if necessary. (If using a food processor, strain off the cooking liquid and reserve. Purée the soup solids with enough cooking liquid to moisten them, then combine with the remaining liquid.)

5 Return the soup to the pan and simmer gently for about 10 minutes to reheat. Ladle into warmed bowls. Garnish with mint leaves.

SERVES 4

70 g/2½ oz sultanas
125 ml/4 fl oz orange juice
1 tbsp olive oil
1 large onion, chopped
250 g/9 oz cabbage, shredded
2 apples, peeled and diced
125 ml/4 fl oz apple juice
400 g/14 oz canned peeled tomatoes
225 ml/8 fl oz tomato or vegetable juice
100 g/3½ oz pineapple flesh, chopped finely
1.2 litres/2 pints water
2 tsp wine vinegar
salt and pepper
fresh mint leaves, to garnish

NUTRITION
Calories *103*; Sugars *24 g*; Protein *2 g*;
Carbohydrate *25 g*; Fat *2 g*; Saturates *0 g*

 easy
 25 mins
 1 hr 30 mins

COOK'S TIP

You can use green or white cabbage to make this soup, but red cabbage would require a much longer cooking. Savoy cabbage has too powerful a flavour.

This soup has a real Mediterranean flavour, using sweet red peppers, tomato, chilli and basil. It is great served with a warm olive bread.

Red Pepper Soup

SERVES 4

225 g/8 oz red peppers, deseeded and sliced
1 onion, sliced
2 garlic cloves, crushed
1 fresh green chilli, chopped
300 m/10 fl oz passata
600 ml/1 pint vegetable stock
2 tbsp chopped fresh basil
fresh basil sprigs, to garnish

1 Put the red peppers in a large, heavy-based pan with the onion, garlic and chilli. Add the passata and vegetable stock and bring to the boil over a medium heat, stirring constantly.

2 Reduce the heat to low and simmer for 20 minutes or until the peppers have softened. Drain, reserving the liquid and vegetables separately.

3 Sieve the vegetables by pressing through a strainer with the back of a spoon. Alternatively, process in a food processor to a smooth purée.

4 Return the vegetable purée to a clean pan and add the reserved cooking liquid. Add the basil and heat through until hot. Garnish the soup with fresh basil sprigs and serve.

NUTRITION

Calories 55; Sugars 10 g; Protein 2 g;
Carbohydrate 11 g; Fat 0.5 g; Saturates 0.1 g

⭐ very easy

🕐 5 mins

🕐 25 mins

 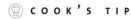 **COOK'S TIP**

This soup is also delicious served cold with 150 ml/5 fl oz natural yogurt swirled into it.

This delicious soup is a wonderful blend of colours and flavours. It is very hot, so if you prefer a milder taste, omit the seeds from the chillies.

Chilli *and* Watercress Soup

1 Put all the ingredients for the stock into a saucepan and bring to the boil.

2 Simmer the stock for 5 minutes. Remove from the heat and strain, reserving the stock.

3 Heat the sunflower oil in a wok or large, heavy frying pan and cook the tofu over a high heat for about 2 minutes, stirring constantly so that the tofu cooks evenly on both sides. Add the strained stock to the wok or pan.

4 Add the mushrooms and coriander and simmer for 3 minutes.

5 Add the watercress and simmer for a further 1 minute.

6 Serve immediately, garnished with red chilli slices.

SERVES 4

1 tbsp sunflower oil
250 g/9 oz smoked tofu, sliced
85 g/3 oz shiitake mushrooms, sliced
2 tbsp chopped fresh coriander
125 g/4½ oz watercress
1 red chilli, sliced finely, to garnish

stock

1 tbsp tamarind pulp
2 dried red chillies, chopped
2 kaffir lime leaves, torn in half
2.5-cm/1-inch piece root ginger, chopped
5-cm/2-inch piece galangal, chopped
1 stalk lemon grass, chopped
1 onion, quartered
1 litre/1¾ pints cold water

NUTRITION
Calories *90*; Sugars *1 g*; Protein *7 g*;
Carbohydrate *2 g*; Fat *6 g*; Saturates *1 g*

 moderate

 10 mins

10 mins

15 mins

🍳 COOK'S TIP

You might like to try a mixture of different types of mushroom. Oyster, button and straw mushrooms are all suitable.

Chinese mushrooms add a unique intense flavour to this soup. Try to obtain them if you can, otherwise use open-cap mushrooms, sliced.

Chilli Fish Soup

SERVES 4

15 g/½ oz Chinese dried mushrooms
2 tbsp sunflower oil
1 onion, sliced
100 g/3½ oz mangetout
100 g/3½ oz bamboo shoots
3 tbsp sweet chilli sauce
1.2 litres/2 pints fish or vegetable stock
3 tbsp light soy sauce
2 tbsp fresh coriander
450 g/1 lb cod fillet, skinned and cubed

1 Place the mushrooms in a large bowl. Pour over enough boiling water to cover and leave to stand for 5 minutes. Drain the mushrooms thoroughly. Using a sharp knife, roughly chop the mushrooms.

2 Heat the sunflower oil in a preheated wok. Add the onion to the wok and stir-fry for 5 minutes or until softened.

3 Add the mangetout, bamboo shoots, chilli sauce, stock and soy sauce to the wok and bring to the boil.

4 Add the coriander and cubed fish to the wok. Leave to simmer for 5 minutes or until the fish is cooked through.

5 Transfer the soup to warmed bowls, garnish with extra coriander, if wished, and serve hot.

NUTRITION

Calories *166*; Sugars *1 g*; Protein *23 g*;
Carbohydrate *4 g*; Fat *7 g*; Saturates *1 g*

  easy

  15 mins

15 mins

🍳 COOK'S TIP

There are many different varieties of dried mushrooms, but shiitake are best. They are not cheap, but a small amount will go a long way.

This is a deliciously different fish soup which can be made quickly and easily in a microwave.

Oriental Fish Soup

1 Beat the egg with the sesame seeds and salt and pepper. Lightly oil a plate and pour on the egg mixture. Cook in a microwave on High power for 1½ minutes until just setting in the centre. Leave to stand for a few minutes, then remove from the plate. Roll up the egg and shred thinly.

2 Mix together the celery, carrot, spring onions and oil in a microwave dish. Cover and cook on High power for 3 minutes.

3 Wash the spinach thoroughly under cold, running water. Cut off and discard any long stalks and drain well. Shred the spinach finely.

4 Add the hot stock, soy sauce, haddock and spinach to the vegetable mixture. Cover and cook on High power for 5 minutes. Stir the soup and season to taste. Serve in warmed bowls with the shredded egg scattered over.

SERVES 4

1 egg
1 tsp sesame seeds, toasted
1 celery stick, chopped
1 carrot, cut into julienne strips
4 spring onions, sliced on the diagonal
1 tbsp oil
60 g/2 oz fresh spinach
850 ml/1½ pints hot vegetable stock
4 tsp light soy sauce
250 g/9 oz haddock, skinned and cut into small chunks
salt and pepper

NUTRITION

Calories *105*; Sugars *1 g*; Protein *13 g*; Carbohydrate *1 g*; Fat *5 g*; Saturates *1 g*

 easy

20 mins

10 mins

COOK'S TIP

Instead of topping the soup with omelette shreds, you could pour the beaten egg, without the sesame seeds, into the hot stock at the end of the cooking time. The egg will set in pretty strands to give a flowery look.

This soup is topped with small wontons filled with prawns, making it both very tasty and satisfying.

Fish Soup *with* Wontons

SERVES 4

125 g/4½ oz large, cooked, peeled prawns
1 tsp chopped chives
1 small garlic clove, chopped finely
1 tbsp vegetable oil
12 wonton wrappers
1 small egg, beaten
850 ml/1½ pints fish stock
175 g/6 oz white fish fillet, diced
dash of chilli sauce
sliced fresh red chilli and chives, to garnish

1 Roughly chop a quarter of the prawns and mix together with the chopped chives and garlic.

2 Heat the oil in a preheated wok or large frying pan until it is really hot.

3 Stir-fry the prawn mixture for 1–2 minutes. Remove from the heat and set aside to cool completely.

4 Spread out the wonton wrappers on a work surface. Spoon a little of the prawn filling into the centre of each wrapper. Brush the edges of the wrappers with beaten egg and press the edges together, scrunching them to form a 'moneybag' shape. Set aside while you are preparing the soup.

5 Pour the fish stock into a large saucepan and bring to the boil. Add the diced white fish and the remaining prawns and cook for 5 minutes.

6 Season to taste with the chilli sauce. Add the wontons and cook for a further 5 minutes.

7 Spoon into warmed serving bowls, garnish with sliced red chilli and chives and serve immediately.

NUTRITION
Calories *115*; Sugars *0 g*; Protein *16 g*;
Carbohydrate *1 g*; Fat *5 g*; Saturates *1 g*

moderate

10 mins

15 mins

COOK'S TIP

Replace the prawns with cooked crabmeat for an alternative flavour.

Ideally, use raw prawns in this soup. If that is not possible, add ready-cooked ones at the very last stage.

Three-flavour Soup

1 Using a sharp knife or meat cleaver, thinly slice the chicken into small shreds. If the prawns are large, cut each in half lengthways, otherwise leave them whole.

2 Place the chicken and prawns in a bowl and mix with a pinch of salt, the egg white and cornflour paste until well coated. Set aside until required.

3 Cut the honey-roast ham into small thin slices roughly the same size as the chicken pieces.

4 In a preheated wok or large, heavy frying pan, bring the Chinese stock or water to a rolling boil and add the chicken, the raw prawns and the ham.

5 Bring the soup back to the boil and simmer for 1 minute.

6 Adjust the seasoning to taste, then pour the soup into four warmed individual serving bowls, garnish with the spring onions and serve immediately.

SERVES 4

125 g/4½ oz skinned, boned chicken breast
125 g/4½ oz raw, peeled prawns
salt
½ egg white, lightly beaten
2 tsp cornflour paste (see page 15)
125 g/4½ oz honey-roast ham
700 ml/1¼ pints Chinese stock
   (see page 15) or water
spring onions, chopped finely, to garnish

NUTRITION
Calories 117; Sugars 0 g; Protein 20 g;
Carbohydrate 2 g; Fat 3 g; Saturates 1 g

easy

3 hrs 30 mins

10 mins

🍳 COOK'S TIP

Soups such as this are improved enormously in flavour if you use a well-flavoured stock. Either use a stock cube, or make Chinese stock (see page 15). Better still, make double quantities and freeze some for future use.

As taste and tolerance for chillies varies, using chilli purée instead of fresh chillies offers more control of the heat.

Thai-style Seafood Soup

SERVES 4

1.2 litres/2 pints fish stock
1 lemon grass stalk, split lengthways
pared rind of ½ lime or 1 lime leaf
2.5 cm/1 inch piece of fresh root ginger, sliced
¼ tsp chilli purée
4–6 spring onions
200 g/7 oz large or medium raw prawns, peeled and deveined
250 g/9 oz scallops (about 16–20)
2 tbsp fresh coriander leaves
salt
red pepper, chopped finely, or fresh red chilli rings, to garnish

1 Put the stock in a pan with the lemon grass, lime rind, ginger and chilli purée. Bring just to the boil, reduce the heat, cover and simmer for 10–15 minutes.

2 Cut the spring onions in half lengthways, then slice crossways very thinly. Cut the prawns almost in half lengthways, keeping the tails intact.

3 Strain the stock, return to the pan and bring to a simmer, with bubbles rising at the edges and the surface trembling. Add the spring onions and cook for 2–3 minutes. Taste and season with salt, if needed, and stir in a little more chilli purée if wished.

4 Add the scallops and prawns and poach for about 1 minute or until they turn opaque and the prawns curl.

5 Add the coriander leaves, ladle the soup into warmed bowls and garnish with red pepper or chillies.

NUTRITION
Calories *132*; Sugars *7 g*; Protein *20 g*;
Carbohydrate *9 g*; Fat *2 g*; Saturates *0 g*

 moderate

10 mins

20 mins

🍲 **COOK'S TIP**

Substitute very small baby leeks, slivered or thinly sliced diagonally, for the spring onions. Include the green parts.

Use prawn, squid or scallops, or a combination of all three, in this healthy soup.

Seafood *and* Tofu Soup

1 Small prawns can be left whole; larger ones should be cut into smaller pieces; cut the squid and scallops into small pieces.

2 If raw, mix the prawns and scallops with the egg white and cornflour paste to prevent them from becoming tough when they are cooked. Cut the cake of tofu into about 24 small cubes.

3 Bring the stock to a rolling boil. Add the tofu and soy sauce, bring back to the boil and simmer for 1 minute.

4 Stir in the seafood, raw pieces first, pre-cooked ones last. Bring back to the boil and simmer for just 1 minute.

5 Adjust the seasoning to taste and serve, garnished with coriander leaves, if liked.

SERVES 4

250 g/9 oz seafood: peeled prawns, squid, scallops, etc., defrosted if frozen
½ egg white, lightly beaten
1 tbsp cornflour paste (see page 15)
1 cake tofu
700 ml/1¼ pints Chinese stock
1 tbsp light soy sauce
salt and pepper
fresh coriander leaves, to garnish (optional)

NUTRITION
Calories *97*; Sugars *0 g*; Protein *17 g*;
Carbohydrate *3 g*; Fat *2 g*; Saturates *0.4 g*

✪✪✪ moderate
🕐 3 hrs 30 mins
🕐 10 mins

 COOK'S TIP

Tofu, also known as bean curd, is made from puréed yellow soya beans, which are very high in protein. Although almost tasteless, tofu absorbs the flavours of other ingredients. It is widely available in supermarkets.

Aromatic lime leaves are used as a flavouring in this soup to add tartness.

Spicy Prawn Soup

SERVES 4

2 tbsp tamarind paste
4 fresh red chillies, chopped very finely
2 garlic cloves, crushed
2 tsp fresh root ginger, chopped finely
4 tbsp fish sauce
2 tbsp palm sugar or caster sugar
1.25 litres/2 pints fish stock
8 lime leaves, roughly torn
100 g/3½ oz carrots, sliced thinly
350 g/12 oz sweet potato, diced
100 g/3½ oz baby corn cobs, halved
3 tbsp roughly chopped fresh coriander
100 g/3½ oz cherry tomatoes, halved
225 g/8 oz raw medium prawns

1 Place the tamarind paste, red chillies, garlic, ginger, fish sauce, palm sugar and fish stock in a preheated wok or large, heavy-based saucepan. Add the lime leaves to the wok. Bring to the boil, stirring constantly, to blend the flavours.

2 Reduce the heat and add the carrots, sweet potato and baby corn cobs to the mixture in the wok.

3 Leave the soup to simmer, uncovered, for about 10 minutes or until the vegetables are just tender.

4 Stir the coriander, cherry tomatoes and prawns into the soup and heat through for 5 minutes or until the prawns have turned pink and opaque.

5 Transfer to a warm soup tureen or individual serving bowls and serve immediately.

NUTRITION
Calories *217*; Sugars *16 g*; Protein *16 g*;
Carbohydrate *31 g*; Fat *4 g*; Saturates *1 g*

very easy

10 mins

20 mins

🍜 **COOK'S TIP**

You could use Thai ginger or galangal, a member of the ginger family, instead of the root ginger in this recipe. It is yellow in colour with pink sprouts and a knobbly surface. The flavour is aromatic and less pungent than ginger.

Crab and sweetcorn are classic ingredients in Chinese cookery. Here, egg noodles are added for a filling dish.

Crab *and* Sweetcorn Soup

1 Heat the sunflower oil in a preheated wok or large, heavy-based saucepan.

2 Add the Chinese five-spice powder, carrots, sweetcorn, peas, spring onions and chilli to the wok and cook for about 5 minutes, stirring constantly.

3 Add the crabmeat to the wok and stir-fry the mixture for 1 minute, distributing the crab evenly.

4 Roughly break up the egg noodles and add to the wok.

5 Pour the fish stock and soy sauce into the wok and bring to the boil.

6 Cover the wok or frying pan and leave the soup to simmer for 5 minutes.

7 Stir once more, then transfer the soup to a warm soup tureen or individual serving bowls and serve immediately.

SERVES 4

1 tbsp sunflower oil
1 tsp Chinese five-spice powder
225 g/8 oz carrots, cut into sticks
150 g/5½ oz canned or frozen sweetcorn
75 g/2¾ oz frozen peas
6 spring onions, trimmed and sliced
1 fresh red chilli, deseeded and sliced very thinly
400 g/14 oz canned white crabmeat
175 g/6 oz egg noodles
1.7 litres/3 pints fish stock
3 tbsp soy sauce

NUTRITION
Calories *324*; Sugars *6 g*; Protein *27 g*; Carbohydrate *39 g*; Fat *8 g*; Saturates *2 g*

✪✪   easy

🕒   5 mins

🕒   20 mins

 COOK'S TIP

Chinese five-spice powder is a mixture of star anise, fennel, cloves, cinnamon and Szechuan pepper. It has an unmistakable flavour. Use it sparingly, as it is very pungent.

Thin strips of beef are marinated in soy sauce and garlic to form the basis of this delicious soup. Served with noodles, it is both filling and delicious.

Beef Noodle Soup

SERVES 4

225 g/8 oz lean beef
1 garlic clove, crushed
2 spring onions, chopped
3 tbsp soy sauce
1 tsp sesame oil
225 g/8 oz egg noodles
850 ml/1½ pints beef stock
3 baby corn cobs, sliced
½ leek, shredded
125 g/4½ oz broccoli, cut into florets
pinch of chilli powder

1 Using a sharp knife, cut the beef into thin strips and place in a bowl with the garlic, spring onions, soy sauce and sesame oil.

2 Combine the ingredients in the bowl, turning the beef to coat. Cover and set aside to marinate in the refrigerator for 30 minutes.

3 Cook the noodles in a pan of boiling water for 3–4 minutes. Drain thoroughly and set aside.

4 Put the beef stock in a large pan and bring to the boil. Add the beef, with the marinade, the baby corn, shredded leek and broccoli florets. Cover and simmer over a low heat for 7–10 minutes or until the beef and vegetables are tender and cooked through.

5 Stir in the noodles and chilli powder and cook for a further 2–3 minutes.

6 Transfer the soup to warmed bowls and serve immediately.

NUTRITION

Calories *186*; Sugars *1 g*; Protein *17 g*; Carbohydrate *20 g*; Fat *5 g*; Saturates *1 g*

 easy

35 mins

20 mins

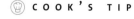 **COOK'S TIP**

Vary the vegetables used or use those to hand. If preferred, use a few drops of chilli sauce instead of chilli powder, but remember it is very hot!

In this recipe the pork is seasoned with traditional Chinese flavourings – soy sauce, rice wine vinegar and a dash of sesame oil.

Chinese Potato *and* Pork Broth

1 Place the chicken stock, diced potatoes and 1 tbsp of the rice wine vinegar in a saucepan and bring to the boil. Reduce the heat until the stock is just simmering.

2 Mix the cornflour with the water, then stir into the hot stock.

3 Bring the stock back to the boil, stirring until thickened, then reduce the heat until it is just simmering again.

4 Place the pork slices in a dish and season with the remaining rice wine vinegar, the soy sauce and sesame oil.

5 Add the pork slices, carrot strips and ginger to the stock and cook for 10 minutes. Stir in the spring onions, red pepper and bamboo shoots. Cook for a further 5 minutes. Pour the soup into warmed bowls and serve immediately.

SERVES 4

1 litre/1¾ pints chicken stock
2 large potatoes, diced
2 tbsp rice wine vinegar
2 tbsp cornflour
4 tbsp water
125 g/4½ oz pork fillet, sliced
1 tbsp light soy sauce
1 tsp sesame oil
1 carrot, cut into very thin strips
1 tsp chopped root ginger
3 spring onions, sliced thinly
1 red pepper, sliced
225 g/8 oz canned bamboo shoots, drained

NUTRITION
Calories *166*; Sugars *2 g*; Protein *10 g*; Carbohydrate *26 g*; Fat *5 g*; Saturates *1 g*

easy

5 mins

20 mins

COOK'S TIP

For extra heat, add 1 chopped red chilli or 1 teaspoon of chilli powder to the soup in step 5.

This meaty chilli tastes lighter than one made with beef. Good for informal entertaining, the recipe is easily doubled.

Pork Chilli Soup

SERVES 4

2 tsp olive oil
500 g/1 lb 2 oz lean minced pork
1 onion, chopped finely
1 celery stick, chopped finely
1 pepper, deseeded and chopped finely
2–3 garlic cloves, chopped finely
400 g/14 oz canned chopped tomatoes in juice
3 tbsp tomato purée
450 ml/16 fl oz chicken or meat stock
¼ tsp ground coriander
¼ tsp ground cumin
¼ tsp dried oregano
1 tsp mild chilli powder
salt and pepper
chopped fresh coriander leaves or parsley, to garnish
soured cream, to serve

1 Heat the oil in a large pan over a medium-high heat. Add the pork, season with salt and pepper, and cook, stirring frequently, until no longer pink. Reduce the heat to medium and add the onion, celery, pepper and garlic. Cover and cook, stirring occasionally, for a further 5 minutes or until the onion is softened.

2 Add the tomatoes, tomato purée and the stock. Stir in the coriander, cumin, oregano and chilli powder. Season with salt and pepper to taste.

3 Bring just to the boil, then reduce the heat to low, cover and simmer for about 30–40 minutes or until all the vegetables are very tender. Taste and adjust the seasoning, adding more chilli powder if you like it hotter.

4 Ladle the chilli into warmed bowls and sprinkle with chopped coriander or parsley. You can either hand round the soured cream separately or top each serving with a spoonful.

NUTRITION

Calories *308*; Sugars *13 g*; Protein *40 g*; Carbohydrate *15 g*; Fat *10 g*; Saturates *3 g*

easy

10 mins

50–60 mins

🍳 **COOK'S TIP**

For extra spicy heat you can replace the mild chilli powder with fresh red or green chillies, chopped finely.

Steaming the meatballs over the soup gives added flavour to the broth. A bamboo steamer that rests on the top of a pan is useful for this recipe.

Oriental Pork Balls *in* Broth

1 To make the pork balls, put the pork, spinach, spring onions and garlic in a bowl. Add the five-spice powder and soy sauce and mix until thoroughly combined.

2 Shape the pork mixture into 24 balls. Place them in a single layer in a steamer that will fit over the top of a pan or in a wok.

3 Bring the stock just to the boil in a pan or wok that will accommodate the steamer. Reduce the heat so that the liquid just bubbles gently. Add the mushrooms to the stock and place the steamer, covered, on top of the pan or wok. Steam for 10 minutes. Remove the steamer and set aside on a plate.

4 Add the pak choi and spring onions to the pan or wok and cook gently in the stock for 3–4 minutes or until the leaves are wilted. Season the broth to taste with salt and pepper.

5 Divide the pork balls between 6 warmed bowls and ladle the soup over them. Serve immediately.

SERVES **6**

2 litres/3½ pints chicken stock
85 g/3 oz shiitake mushrooms, sliced thinly
175 g/6 oz pak choi or other Chinese greens, sliced into thin ribbons
6 spring onions, sliced finely
salt and pepper

pork balls

225 g/8 oz lean minced pork
25 g/1 oz fresh spinach leaves, chopped finely
2 spring onions, chopped finely
1 garlic clove, chopped very finely
pinch of Chinese five-spice powder
1 tsp soy sauce

NUTRITION
Calories *67*; Sugars *1 g*; Protein *9 g*;
Carbohydrate *3 g*; Fat *2 g*; Saturates *1 g*

✪✪✪　　moderate

🖐　　15 mins

🕐　　18 mins

This is a very filling soup, as it contains rice and tender pieces of lamb. Serve before a light main course.

Lamb *and* Rice Soup

SERVES 4

150 g/5½ oz lean boneless lamb
50 g/1¾ oz rice
850 ml/1½ pints lamb stock
1 leek, sliced
1 garlic clove, sliced thinly
2 tsp light soy sauce
1 tsp rice wine vinegar
1 medium open-cap mushroom, sliced thinly
salt

1 Using a sharp knife, trim any fat from the lamb and cut the meat into thin strips. Set aside until required.

2 Bring a pan of lightly salted water to the boil and add the rice. Bring back to the boil, stir once, reduce the heat and cook for 10–15 minutes or until tender.

3 Drain the rice, rinse under cold running water, drain again and set aside until required.

4 Meanwhile, put the lamb stock in a large saucepan and bring to the boil.

5 Add the lamb strips, leek, garlic, soy sauce and rice wine vinegar to the stock in the pan. Reduce the heat, cover and leave to simmer for 10 minutes or until the lamb is tender and cooked through.

6 Add the mushroom slices and the rice to the pan and cook for a further 2–3 minutes or until the mushroom is completely cooked through.

7 Ladle the soup into 4 individual warmed soup bowls and serve immediately.

NUTRITION

Calories *116*; Sugars *0.2 g*; Protein *9 g*; Carbohydrate *12 g*; Fat *4 g*; Saturates *2 g*

easy

5 mins

35 mins

COOK'S TIP

Use a few dried Chinese mushrooms, rehydrated according to the packet instructions and chopped, as an alternative to the open-cap mushroom. Add the Chinese mushrooms with the lamb in step 4.

Packed with tomatoes, chickpeas and vegetables, this thick and hearty main course soup is bursting with exotic flavours and aromas.

Spicy Lamb Soup

1 Heat the oil in a large pan or flameproof casserole over a medium-high heat. Add the lamb, in batches if necessary, and cook, stirring occasionally, until evenly browned on all sides, adding a little more oil if needed. Remove the meat with a draining spoon and set aside.

2 Reduce the heat and add the onion and garlic to the pan. Cook, stirring frequently, for 1–2 minutes.

3 Add the water and return all the meat to the pan. Bring just to the boil and skim off any foam that rises to the surface. Reduce the heat and stir in the tomatoes, bay leaf, thyme, oregano, cinnamon, cumin, turmeric and harissa. Simmer for about 1 hour or until the meat is very tender. Discard the bay leaf.

4 Stir in the chick peas, carrot and potato and simmer for 15 minutes. Add the courgette and peas and simmer for a further 15–20 minutes or until all the vegetables are tender.

5 Season to taste with salt and pepper and add more harissa if desired. Ladle the soup into warmed bowls, garnish with chopped fresh mint or coriander and serve immediately.

SERVES 4

1–2 tbsp olive oil
450 g/1 lb lean boneless lamb, such as shoulder or neck fillet, trimmed of fat and cut into 1-cm/½-inch cubes
1 onion, chopped finely
2–3 garlic cloves, crushed
1.2 litres/2 pints water
400 g/14 oz canned chopped tomatoes in juice
1 bay leaf
½ tsp dried thyme
½ tsp dried oregano
pinch of ground cinnamon
¼ tsp ground cumin
¼ tsp ground turmeric
1 tsp harissa
400 g/14 oz canned chickpeas, rinsed and drained
1 carrot, diced
1 potato, diced
1 courgette, quartered lengthways and sliced
100 g/3½ oz fresh or frozen green peas
salt and pepper
mint or coriander leaves, to garnish

NUTRITION

Calories 323; Sugars 6 g; Protein 27 g; Carbohydrate 25 g; Fat 13 g; Saturates 4 g

✪✪✪   moderate

🕐   10 mins

    1 hr 45 mins

Tender cooked chicken strips and baby corn cobs are the main flavours in this delicious clear soup, with just a hint of ginger.

Curried Chicken Soup

SERVES 4

175 g/6 oz canned sweetcorn, drained

850 ml/1½ pints chicken stock

350 g/12 oz cooked, lean chicken, cut into strips

16 baby corn cobs

1 tsp Chinese curry powder

1 cm/½ inch piece of fresh root ginger, grated

3 tbsp light soy sauce

2 tbsp chopped fresh chives

1 Place the canned sweetcorn in a food processor, with 150 ml/5 fl oz of the chicken stock and process until the mixture forms a smooth purée.

2 Pass the sweetcorn purée through a fine sieve, pressing with the back of a spoon to remove any husks.

3 Pour the remaining chicken stock into a large pan and add the strips of cooked chicken. Stir in the sweetcorn purée to combine.

4 Add the baby corn cobs and bring the soup to the boil. Boil over a medium heat for 10 minutes.

5 Add the Chinese curry powder, grated fresh root ginger and light soy sauce and stir well to combine. Cook for a further 10–15 minutes.

6 Stir in the chopped chives. Transfer the soup to warmed soup bowls and serve immediately.

NUTRITION

Calories 206; Sugars 5 g; Protein 29 g; Carbohydrate 13 g; Fat 5 g; Saturates 1 g

easy

5 mins

30 mins

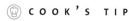 COOK'S TIP

Prepare the soup up to 24 hours in advance without adding the chicken. Cool, cover and store in the refrigerator. Add the chicken and heat the soup through thoroughly before serving.

This tasty chicken soup has the addition of poached eggs, making it both delicious and filling. Use fresh, home-made stock for a better flavour.

Clear Chicken *and* Egg Soup

1 Bring a large saucepan of water to the boil and add the salt and rice wine vinegar.

2 Reduce the heat so that it is just simmering and carefully break the eggs into the water, one at a time. Poach the eggs for 1 minute.

3 Remove the poached eggs with a slotted spoon and set aside.

4 Bring the chicken stock to the boil in a separate pan and add the leek, broccoli, chicken, mushrooms and sherry and season with chilli sauce to taste. Cook for 10–15 minutes.

5 Add the poached eggs to the soup and cook for a further 2 minutes. Carefully transfer the soup and poached eggs to 4 soup bowls. Dust with a little chilli powder and serve immediately.

SERVES 4

1 tsp salt
1 tbsp rice wine vinegar
4 eggs
850 ml/1½ pints chicken stock
1 leek, sliced
125 g/4½ oz broccoli florets
125 g/4½ oz shredded cooked chicken
2 open-cap mushrooms, sliced
1 tbsp dry sherry
dash of chilli sauce
chilli powder, to garnish

NUTRITION
Calories *138*; Sugars *1 g*; Protein *16 g*; Carbohydrate *1 g*; Fat *7 g*; Saturates *2 g*

⭐⭐   easy

🕐   5 mins

🕐   35 mins

 COOK'S TIP

You could use 4 dried Chinese mushrooms, rehydrated according to the packet instructions, instead of the open-cap mushrooms, if you prefer.

This filling soup is packed with spicy flavours and bright colours for a really attractive and hearty dish.

Spicy Chicken Noodle Soup

SERVES 4

2 tbsp tamarind paste
4 red chillies, chopped finely
2 garlic cloves, crushed
2 tsp finely chopped fresh root ginger
4 tbsp fish sauce
2 tbsp palm sugar or caster sugar
8 lime leaves, roughly torn
1.2 litres/2 pints chicken stock
350 g/12 oz boneless, skinless chicken breast
100 g/3½ oz carrots, sliced thinly
350 g/12 oz sweet potato, diced
100 g/3½ oz baby corn cobs, halved
3 tbsp roughly chopped fresh coriander
100 g/3½ oz cherry tomatoes, halved
150 g/5½ oz flat rice noodles
chopped fresh coriander, to garnish

1 Preheat a large wok or frying pan. Place the tamarind paste, chillies, garlic, ginger, fish sauce, sugar, lime leaves and chicken stock in the wok and bring to the boil, stirring constantly. Reduce the heat and cook for about 5 minutes.

2 Using a sharp knife, thinly slice the chicken. Add the chicken to the wok and cook for a further 5 minutes, stirring the mixture well.

3 Add the carrots, sweet potato and baby corn cobs to the wok. Leave to simmer, uncovered, for 5 minutes or until the vegetables are just tender and the chicken is completely cooked through.

4 Stir in the chopped fresh coriander, cherry tomatoes and flat rice noodles.

5 Leave the soup to simmer for about 5 minutes or until the noodles are tender.

6 Garnish the spicy chicken noodle soup with chopped fresh coriander and serve hot.

NUTRITION

Calories *286*; Sugars *21 g*; Protein *22 g*; Carbohydrate *37 g*; Fat *6 g*; Saturates *1 g*

  easy

15 mins

20 mins

🍲 **COOK'S TIP**

Tamarind paste is produced from the seed pod of the tamarind tree. It adds both a brown colour and tang to soups and gravies. If unavailable, dilute molasses (dark muscovado) sugar or treacle with lime juice.

This fragrant soup combines citrus flavours with coconut and a hint of piquancy from chillies.

Chicken *and* Coconut Soup

1 Using a sharp knife, slice the chicken into thin strips.

2 Place the coconut in a heatproof bowl and pour over the boiling water. Work the coconut mixture through a sieve. Pour the coconut water into a large saucepan and add the stock.

3 Add the spring onions to the saucepan. Slice the base of each lemon grass stalk and discard any damaged leaves. Bruise the stalks and add to the saucepan.

4 Peel the green rind from the lime in large strips. Squeeze the juice and add to the pan with the lime strips, ginger, soy sauce and coriander. Squash the chillies with a fork then add to the pan. Heat to just below boiling point.

5 Add the chicken and fresh coriander to the saucepan, bring to the boil, then reduce the heat and simmer for 10 minutes.

6 Discard the lemon grass, lime rind and red chillies. Pour the blended cornflour mixture into the saucepan and stir until slightly thickened. Season with salt and white pepper to taste and serve immediately, garnished with chopped red chilli.

SERVES 4

350 g/12 oz cooked, skinned chicken breast
125 g/4½ oz unsweetened desiccated coconut
500 ml/16 fl oz boiling water
500 ml/18 fl oz fresh chicken stock
4 spring onions, white and green parts, sliced thinly
2 stalks lemon grass
1 lime
1 tsp grated root ginger
1 tbsp light soy sauce
2 tsp ground coriander
2 large fresh red chillies
1 tbsp chopped fresh coriander
1 tbsp cornflour, mixed with 2 tbsp cold water
salt and white pepper
chopped red chilli, to garnish

NUTRITION
Calories *345*; Sugars *2 g*; Protein *28 g*; Carbohydrate *5 g*; Fat *24 g*; Saturates *18 g*

⭐⭐⭐ moderate
🕐 2 hrs 15 mins
🕐 15 mins

Make this soup when you want a change from traditional chicken soup. It is nicely spicy. Use a generous amount of fresh coriander leaves to garnish.

Thai-style Chicken *and* Coconut Soup

SERVES 4

1.2 litres/2 pints chicken stock
200 g/7 oz boneless, skinless chicken
1 fresh chilli, split lengthways and deseeded
7.5-cm/3-inch piece lemon grass, split lengthways
3-4 lime leaves
2.5-cm/1-inch piece fresh root ginger, peeled and sliced
125 ml/4 fl oz coconut milk
6-8 spring onions, sliced diagonally
¼ tsp chilli purée, or to taste
salt
fresh coriander leaves, to garnish

1 Put the stock in a pan with the chicken, chilli, lemon grass, lime leaves and ginger. Bring almost to the boil, reduce the heat, cover and simmer for 20–25 minutes or until the chicken is cooked through and firm to the touch.

2 Remove the chicken from the pan and strain the stock. Set aside the chilli and lime leaves. When the chicken is cool, slice thinly or shred into bite-sized pieces.

3 Return the stock to the saucepan and heat to simmering. Stir in the coconut milk and spring onions. Add the chicken and continue simmering for about 10 minutes or until the soup is heated through and the flavours have mingled.

4 Stir in the chilli purée. Season to taste with salt and, if wished, add a little more chilli purée.

5 Ladle into warmed bowls and float fresh coriander leaves, the chilli and the lime leaves on top to serve.

NUTRITION
Calories 76; Sugars 2 g; Protein 13 g; Carbohydrate 3 g; Fat 1 g; Saturates 0 g

easy

5 mins

40 mins

🕮 **COOK'S TIP**

Once the stock is flavoured and the chicken cooked, this soup is very quick to finish. If you wish, poach the chicken and strain the stock ahead of time. Store in the refrigerator separately.

This well-known soup from Peking is easy to make and very filling. It is often eaten as a meal on its own and should be served before a light menu if it is offered as an appetizer.

Hot *and* Sour Soup

1 Blend the cornflour with the water to form a smooth paste. Add the soy sauce, rice wine vinegar, pepper and chilli and mix together well.

2 Break the egg into a separate bowl and beat well.

3 Heat the oil in a preheated wok and fry the onion for 1–2 minutes.

4 Stir in the stock, mushroom and chicken and bring to the boil. Cook for about 15 minutes or until the chicken is tender.

5 Pour the cornflour mixture into the soup and cook, stirring constantly, until it thickens.

6 As you are stirring, gradually drizzle the egg into the soup, to create threads of egg.

7 Sprinkle with the sesame oil and serve immediately.

SERVES 4

2 tbsp cornflour
4 tbsp water
2 tbsp light soy sauce
3 tbsp rice wine vinegar
1/2 tsp ground black pepper
1 small fresh red chilli, chopped finely
1 egg
2 tbsp vegetable oil
1 onion, chopped
850 ml/1 1/2 pints chicken or beef stock
1 open-cap mushroom, sliced
50 g/1 3/4 oz skinless, boneless chicken breast, cut into very thin strips
1 tsp sesame oil

NUTRITION
Calories *124*; Sugars *1 g*; Protein *5 g*; Carbohydrate *8 g*; Fat *8 g*; Saturates *1 g*

 moderate
 3 hrs 30 mins
3 25 mins

🤍 **COOK'S TIP**

Make sure that the egg is poured in very slowly and that you stir continuously to create threads of egg and not large pieces.

How delicious a simple, fresh soup can be. Chicken wings are good to use for making the stock, as the meat is very sweet and doesn't dry out.

Chicken Soup *with* Stars

SERVES 4

85 g/3 oz small pasta stars, or other very small shapes
chopped fresh parsley

chicken stock

1.25 kg/2 lb 12 oz chicken pieces, such as wings or legs
2.5 litres/4½ pints water
1 celery stick, sliced
1 large carrot, sliced
1 onion, sliced
1 leek, sliced
2 garlic cloves, crushed
8 peppercorns
4 allspice berries
3–4 parsley stems
2–3 fresh thyme sprigs
1 bay leaf
salt and pepper

1 Put the chicken in a large flameproof casserole with the water, celery, carrot, onion, leek, garlic, peppercorns, allspice, herbs and ½ teaspoon salt. Bring just to the boil and skim off the foam that rises to the surface. Reduce the heat, partially cover and simmer for 2 hours.

2 Remove the chicken from the stock and set aside to cool. Continue simmering the stock, uncovered, for about 30 minutes. When the chicken is cool enough to handle, remove the meat from the bones and, if necessary, cut into bite-sized pieces.

3 Strain the stock and remove as much fat as possible. Discard the vegetables and flavourings. (There should be about 1.8 litres/3 pints chicken stock.)

4 Bring the stock to the boil in a clean pan. Add the pasta and reduce the heat so that the stock boils very gently. Cook for about 10 minutes or until the pasta is tender, but still firm to the bite.

5 Stir in the chicken meat. Taste the soup and adjust the seasoning if necessary. Ladle into warmed bowls and serve sprinkled with parsley.

NUTRITION

Calories *119*; Sugars *2 g*; Protein *14 g*; Carbohydrate *13 g*; Fat *2 g*; Saturates *0 g*

moderate

20 mins

2 hrs 45 mins

This soup is a good way of using up leftover cooked chicken and rice. Any kind of rice is suitable, from white or brown long-grain rice to wild rice.

Chicken *and* Rice Soup

1 Put the stock in a large saucepan and add the carrots, celery and leek. Bring to the boil, reduce the heat to low and simmer gently, partially covered, for 10 minutes.

2 Stir in the peas, rice and chicken and continue cooking for a further 10–15 minutes or until the vegetables are tender.

3 Add the chopped tarragon and parsley, then taste and adjust the seasoning, adding salt and pepper as needed.

4 Ladle the soup into warmed bowls, garnish with parsley and serve.

SERVES 4

1.5 litres/2¾ pints chicken stock (see Cook's Tip)
2 small carrots, sliced very thinly
1 celery stick, diced finely
1 baby leek, halved lengthways and sliced thinly
115 g/4 oz tiny peas, defrosted if frozen
175 g/6 oz cooked rice
150 g/5½ oz cooked chicken, sliced
2 tsp chopped fresh tarragon
1 tbsp chopped fresh parsley
salt and pepper
fresh parsley sprigs, to garnish

NUTRITION
Calories *165*; Sugars *3 g*; Protein *14 g*; Carbohydrate *19 g*; Fat *4 g*; Saturates *1 g*

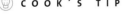 **COOK'S TIP**

If the stock you are using is a little weak, or if you have used a stock cube, add the herbs at the beginning, so that they can flavour the stock for a longer time.

 very easy

25 mins

30 mins

This is a hearty and
robustly flavoured soup,
containing pieces of duck
and vegetables cooked
in a rich stock.

Peking Duck Soup

SERVES 4

115 g/4 oz lean duck breast meat
225 g/8 oz Chinese leaves
850 ml/1½ pints chicken or duck stock
1 tbsp dry sherry or Chinese rice wine
1 tbsp light soy sauce
2 garlic cloves, crushed
pinch of ground star anise
1 tbsp sesame seeds
1 tsp sesame oil
1 tbsp chopped fresh parsley

1 Remove the skin from the duck breast and finely dice the flesh. Using a sharp knife, shred the Chinese leaves.

2 Put the stock in a large pan and bring to the boil over a medium heat. Add the sherry or rice wine, soy sauce, diced duck meat and shredded Chinese leaves and stir thoroughly. Reduce the heat and simmer gently for 15 minutes.

3 Stir in the garlic and star anise and cook over a low heat for a further 10–15 minutes or until the duck is tender.

4 Meanwhile, dry-fry the sesame seeds in a preheated, heavy-based frying pan or wok, stirring constantly until they give off their fragrance.

5 Remove the sesame seeds from the pan and stir them into the soup, with the sesame oil and the chopped fresh parsley.

6 Ladle the Peking duck soup into warmed bowls and serve immediately.

NUTRITION
Calories *92*; Sugars *3 g*; Protein *8 g*;
Carbohydrate *3 g*; Fat *5 g*; Saturates *1 g*

⊛⊛⊛   moderate

⊘   5 mins

◷   35 mins

👒 **COOK'S TIP**

If Chinese leaves are unavailable, use leafy green cabbage instead. You may wish to adjust the quantity to taste, as Western cabbage has a stronger flavour and aroma than Chinese leaves.

This soup combines delicate flavours with a satisfying meaty taste. Although duck is notoriously fatty, the legs are leaner than the breast.

Oriental Duck Broth

1 Put the duck in a large pan with the water. Bring just to the boil and skim off the foam that rises to the surface. Add the stock, ginger, sliced carrot, leek and onion, garlic, peppercorns and soy sauce. Reduce the heat, partially cover and simmer gently for 1½ hours.

2 Remove the duck from the stock and set aside. When the duck is cool enough to handle, remove the meat from the bones and slice thinly or shred into bite-sized pieces, discarding any fat.

3 Strain the stock and press with the back of a spoon to extract all the liquid. Remove as much fat as possible. Discard the vegetables and flavourings.

4 Bring the stock just to the boil in a clean saucepan and add the strips of carrot and leek and the mushrooms with the duck meat. Reduce the heat and simmer gently for 5 minutes or until the carrot is just tender.

5 Stir in the watercress and continue simmering for 1–2 minutes or until it is wilted. Taste the soup and adjust the seasoning if necessary, adding a little more soy sauce if wished. Ladle the soup into warmed soup bowls and serve immediately.

SERVES 4

2 duck leg quarters, skinned
1 litre/1¾ pints water
600 ml/1 pint chicken stock
2.5-cm/1-inch piece of fresh root ginger, sliced
1 large carrot, sliced
1 leek, sliced
1 onion, sliced
3 garlic cloves, crushed
l tsp black peppercorns
2 tbsp soy sauce
I small carrot, cut into thin strips or slivers
I small leek, cut into thin strips or slivers
100 g/3½ oz shiitake mushrooms, sliced thinly
25 g/1 oz watercress leaves
salt and pepper

NUTRITION
Calories *98*; Sugars *4 g*; Protein *9 g*; Carbohydrate *9 g*; Fat *3 g*; Saturates *1 g*

⭐⭐ easy

🕐 10 mins

🕐 1 hr 45 mins

European Soups

Soups are an important part of Mediterranean cuisine and vary in content from hearty bean concoctions suitable for the coldest winter's day to creamy Vichyssoise and meaty stews. In this chapter there are nourishing lentil soup recipes, variations on minestrone soup and thick fish soups. Dishes include Gazpacho from Spain, Beef Goulash Soup from Hungary and an Italian Brown Lentil and Pasta Soup. Many of these soups are suitable for a main-course meal when combined with delicious freshly baked bread.

Plum tomatoes are ideal
for making soups and
sauces as they have denser,
less watery flesh than
rounder varieties.

Tomato *and* Pasta Soup

SERVES 4

60 g/2 oz unsalted butter
1 large onion, chopped
600 ml/1 pint vegetable stock
900 g/2 lb Italian plum tomatoes,
    peeled and chopped roughly
pinch of bicarbonate of soda
225 g/8 oz dried fusilli
1 tbsp caster sugar
150 ml/5 floz double cream
salt and pepper
fresh basil leaves, to garnish

1 Melt the butter in a large pan, add the onion and fry for 3 minutes, stirring. Add 300 ml/$\frac{1}{2}$ pint of vegetable stock to the pan, with the chopped tomatoes and bicarbonate of soda. Bring the soup to the boil and simmer for 20 minutes.

2 Remove the pan from the heat and set aside to cool a little. Purée the soup in a blender or food processor, then pour it through a fine sieve back into the saucepan.

3 Add the remaining vegetable stock and the fusilli to the pan, and season to taste with salt and pepper.

4 Add the sugar to the pan, bring to the boil, then reduce the heat and simmer for about 15 minutes.

5 Pour the soup into a warm tureen or individual warmed bowls, swirl the double cream around the surface of the soup and garnish with fresh basil leaves. Serve immediately.

NUTRITION
Calories *503*; Sugars *16 g*; Protein *9 g*;
Carbohydrate *59 g*; Fat *28 g*; Saturates *17 g*

 easy

5 mins

50–55 mins

🍴 **COOK'S TIP**

To make orange and tomato soup, simply use half the quantity of vegetable stock, topped up with the same amount of fresh orange juice, and garnish the soup with orange rind.

This Spanish soup is full of chopped and grated vegetables with a puréed tomato base. It requires chilling, so prepare well in advance.

Gazpacho

1 Coarsely grate the cucumber into a large bowl and add the chopped green pepper.

2 Process the tomatoes, onion and garlic in a food processor or blender, then add the oil, vinegar, lemon or lime juice and tomato purée and process until smooth. Alternatively, finely chop the tomatoes and finely grate the onion, then mix both with the garlic, oil, vinegar, lemon and tomato purée.

3 Add the tomato mixture to the bowl and mix well, then add the tomato juice and mix again.

4 Season to taste, cover the large bowl with cling film and chill thoroughly – for at least 6 hours and preferably longer so that the flavours have time to meld together.

5 Prepare the side dishes of green pepper, onion rings and garlic croûtons, and arrange in individual serving bowls.

6 Ladle the soup into bowls, preferably from a soup tureen set on the table with the side dishes placed around it. Hand the dishes around to allow the guests to help themselves.

SERVES 4

½ small cucumber
½ small green pepper, deseeded and chopped very finely
500 g/1 lb 2 oz ripe tomatoes, peeled or 400 g/14 oz canned chopped tomatoes
½ onion, chopped coarsely
2–3 garlic cloves, crushed
3 tbsp olive oil
2 tbsp white wine vinegar
1–2 tbsp lemon or lime juice
2 tbsp tomato purée
450 ml/16 fl oz tomato juice
salt and pepper

to serve
chopped green pepper
onion rings, sliced thinly
garlic croûtons (see page 89)

NUTRITION

Calories *140*; Sugars *12 g*; Protein *3 g*; Carbohydrate *13 g*; Fat *9 g*; Saturates *1 g*

 very easy

 6 hrs 30 mins

00 mins

A delicious creamy soup with grated carrot and chopped parsley for texture and colour. Serve with crusty cheese scones for a hearty lunch.

Thick Onion Soup

SERVES 6

75 g/2¾ oz butter
500 g/1 lb 2 oz onions, chopped finely
1 garlic clove, crushed
40 g/1½ oz plain flour
600 ml/1 pint vegetable stock
600 ml/1 pint milk
2–3 tsp lemon or lime juice
good pinch of ground allspice
1 bay leaf
1 carrot, grated coarsely
4–6 tbsp double cream
2 tbsp chopped parsley
salt and pepper

cheese scones

225 g/8 oz malted wheat or wholemeal flour
2 tsp baking powder
60 g/2 oz butter
4 tbsp grated Parmesan cheese
1 egg, beaten
about 75 ml/3 fl oz milk

NUTRITION

Calories 277; Sugars 12 g; Protein 6 g;
Carbohydrate 19 g; Fat 20 g; Saturates 8 g

 easy

20 mins

1 hr 10 mins

1 Melt the butter in a saucepan and fry the onions and garlic over a low heat, stirring frequently, for 10–15 minutes or until soft, but not coloured. Stir in the flour and cook, stirring, for 1 minute, then gradually stir in the stock and bring to the boil, stirring frequently. Add the milk, then bring back to the boil.

2 Season to taste with salt and pepper and add 2 teaspoons of the lemon or lime juice, the allspice and bay leaf. Cover and simmer for about 25 minutes or until the vegetables are tender. Discard the bay leaf.

3 Meanwhile, make the scones. Combine the flour and baking powder. Season with salt and pepper and rub in the butter until the mixture resembles fine breadcrumbs. Stir in 3 tablespoons of the cheese, the egg and enough milk to mix to a soft dough.

4 Shape into a bar about 2 cm/¾ inch thick. Place on a floured baking tray and mark into slices. Sprinkle with the remaining cheese and bake in a preheated oven at 220°C/425°F/Gas Mark 7 for about 20 minutes or until risen and golden brown.

5 Stir the carrot into the soup and simmer for 2–3 minutes. Add more lemon or lime juice, if necessary. Stir in the cream and reheat. Garnish with chopped parsley and serve with the warm scones.

Fresh pesto is a treat to the taste buds and very different in flavour from that available from supermarkets. Store fresh pesto in the refrigerator.

Potato *and* Pesto Soup

1 To make the pesto sauce, put all of the ingredients in a blender or food processor and process for 2 minutes, or blend by hand using a pestle and mortar.

2 Finely chop the bacon, potatoes and onions. Heat the oil in a large pan. Fry the bacon over a medium heat for 4 minutes. Add the butter, potatoes and onions and cook for 12 minutes, stirring constantly.

3 Add the stock and milk to the pan, bring to the boil and simmer for 10 minutes. Add the conchigliette and simmer for a further 10-12 minutes.

4 Blend in the cream and simmer for 5 minutes. Add the parsley, salt and pepper and 2 tbsp pesto sauce. Transfer the soup to serving bowls and serve with Parmesan cheese and fresh garlic bread.

SERVES 4

3 slices rindless, smoked, fatty bacon
450 g/1 lb floury potatoes
450 g/ 1 lb onions
2 tbsp olive oil
25 g/1 oz butter
600 ml/1 pint chicken stock
600 ml/1 pint milk
100 g/3½ oz dried conchigliette
150 ml/5 fl oz double cream
chopped fresh parsley
salt and pepper
shaved or freshly grated Parmesan cheese
  and garlic bread, to serve

pesto sauce

60 g/2 oz finely chopped fresh parsley
2 garlic cloves, crushed
60 g/2 oz pine nuts, crushed
2 tbsp chopped fresh basil leaves
60 g/2 oz freshly grated Parmesan cheese
white pepper
150 ml/5 fl oz olive oil

NUTRITION

Calories *548*; Sugars *0 g*; Protein *11 g*; Carbohydrate *10 g*; Fat *52 g*; Saturates *18 g*

✪✪   easy

🕐   5–10 mins

      50 mins

This creamy soup has a delightful pale green colouring and rich flavour from the blend of tender broccoli and blue cheese.

Broccoli *and* Potato Soup

SERVES 4

2 tbsp olive oil
450 g/1 lb potatoes, diced
1 onion, diced
225 g/8 oz broccoli florets
125 g/4½ oz blue cheese, crumbled
1 litre/1¾ pints vegetable stock
150 m/5 fl oz double cream
pinch of paprika
salt and pepper

1 Heat the oil in a large saucepan. Add the potatoes and onion. Sauté, stirring constantly, for 5 minutes.

2 Reserve a few broccoli florets for the garnish and add the remaining broccoli to the pan. Add the cheese and the vegetable stock.

3 Bring to the boil, then reduce the heat, cover the pan and simmer for 25 minutes or until the potatoes are tender.

4 Transfer the soup to a food processor or blender in batches and process until the mixture is smooth. Alternatively, press the vegetables through a sieve with the back of a wooden spoon.

5 Return the purée to a clean saucepan and stir in the double cream and a pinch of paprika. Season to taste with salt and pepper.

6 Blanch the reserved broccoli florets in a little boiling water for about 2 minutes, then lift them out of the pan with a slotted spoon.

7 Pour the soup into warmed individual bowls and garnish with the broccoli florets and a sprinkling of paprika. Serve the soup immediately.

NUTRITION

Calories *452*; Sugars *4 g*; Protein *14 g*; Carbohydrate *20 g*; Fat *35 g*; Saturates *19 g*

 moderate

5–10 mins

35 mins

🍳 COOK'S TIP

This soup freezes very successfully. Follow the method described here up to step 4, and freeze the soup after it has been puréed. Add the cream and paprika just before serving. Garnish and serve.

This refreshing chilled soup is ideal for al fresco dining. It is very quick to make, but needs several hours in the refrigerator to chill thoroughly.

Onion *and* Artichoke Soup

1 Heat the olive oil in a large saucepan and cook the chopped onion and crushed garlic over a medium heat until just softened.

2 Using a sharp knife, roughly chop the artichoke hearts. Add the artichoke pieces to the onion and garlic mixture in the pan. Add the hot vegetable stock to the pan, stirring constantly.

3 Bring the mixture to the boil, then reduce the heat and leave to simmer, covered, for about 3 minutes.

4 Transfer the mixture to a food processor and blend until a smooth purée is formed. Alternatively, push the mixture through a sieve with the back of a wooden spoon.

5 Return the soup to the saucepan. Stir the single cream and fresh thyme into the soup.

6 Transfer the soup to a large bowl, cover and leave to chill in the refrigerator for about 3–4 hours.

7 Transfer the chilled soup to individual soup bowls and garnish with strips of sun-dried tomato. Serve with lots of fresh, crusty bread.

 COOK'S TIP

Try adding 2 tablespoons of dry vermouth, such as Martini, to the soup in step 5 if you wish.

SERVES 4

1 tbsp olive oil
1 onion, chopped
1 garlic clove, crushed
800 g/28 oz canned artichoke hearts, drained
600 ml/1 pint hot vegetable stock
150 ml/5 fl oz single cream
2 tbsp fresh thyme, stalks removed
2 sun-dried tomatoes, cut into strips
fresh crusty bread, to serve

NUTRITION
Calories *159*; Sugars *2 g*; Protein *2 g*; Carbohydrate *5 g*; Fat *15 g*; Saturates *6 g*

✪✪✪   moderate

🕐   5 mins

🕐   15 mins

Mediterranean vegetables, roasted in olive oil and flavoured with thyme, are the basis for this delicious soup.

Roasted Vegetable Soup

SERVES 6

2–3 tbsp olive oil
700 g/1 lb 9 oz ripe tomatoes, peeled, halved and cored
3 large yellow peppers, halved, cored and deseeded
3 courgettes, halved lengthways
1 small aubergine, halved lengthways
4 garlic cloves, halved
2 onions, cut into eighths
pinch of dried thyme
1 litre/1¾ pints vegetable stock
125 ml/4 fl oz single cream
salt and pepper
shredded fresh basil leaves, to garnish

NUTRITION
Calories *163*; Sugars *13 g*; Protein *5 g*;
Carbohydrate *15 g*; Fat *10 g*; Saturates *3 g*

 moderate

 15 mins

1 hr 15 mins

1 Brush a large shallow baking dish with olive oil. Laying them cut-side down, arrange the tomatoes, peppers, courgettes and aubergine in one layer (use two dishes, if necessary). Tuck the garlic cloves and onion pieces into the gaps and drizzle the vegetables with olive oil. Season lightly with salt and pepper and sprinkle with the thyme.

2 Place the vegetables in a preheated oven at 190°C/375°F/Gas Mark 5 and bake, uncovered, for 30–35 minutes or until soft and browned around the edges. Leave to cool, then scrape out the aubergine flesh and remove the skin from the peppers.

3 Working in batches, put the aubergine and pepper flesh, together with the courgettes, into a food processor and chop to the consistency of salsa or pickle; do not purée. Alternatively, place in a bowl and chop together with a knife.

4 Combine the stock with the chopped vegetable mixture in a saucepan and simmer over a medium heat for 20–30 minutes or until all the vegetables are tender and the flavours have completely blended.

5 Stir in the cream and simmer the soup over a low heat for about 5 minutes, stirring occasionally, until hot. Taste and adjust the seasoning, if necessary. Ladle the soup into warmed bowls, garnish with basil and serve.

This is a classic creamy soup made from potatoes and leeks. To achieve the delicate pale colour, be sure to use only the white parts of the leeks.

Vichyssoise

1 Trim the leeks and remove most of the green parts. Slice the white parts of the leeks very finely.

2 Melt the butter or margarine in a saucepan. Add the leeks and onion and cook, stirring occasionally, for about 5 minutes without browning.

3 Add the potatoes, vegetable stock, lemon juice, nutmeg, coriander and bay leaf to the pan, season to taste with salt and pepper and bring to the boil. Cover and simmer for about 30 minutes or until all the vegetables are very soft.

4 Cool the soup a little, remove and discard the bay leaf, then press through a sieve or process in a food processor or blender until smooth. Pour into a clean pan.

5 Blend the egg yolk into the cream, add a little of the soup to the mixture, then whisk it all back into the soup and reheat gently, without boiling. Adjust the seasoning to taste. Leave to cool and then chill thoroughly in the refrigerator.

6 Serve the soup sprinkled with freshly snipped chives.

SERVES 6

3 large leeks
40 g/1½ oz butter or margarine
1 onion, sliced thinly
500 g/1 lb 2 oz potatoes, chopped
850 ml/1½ pints vegetable stock
2 tsp lemon juice
pinch of ground nutmeg
¼ tsp ground coriander
1 bay leaf
1 egg yolk
150 ml/5 fl oz single cream
salt and pepper
freshly snipped chives, to garnish

NUTRITION
Calories *208*; Sugars *5 g*; Protein *5 g*;
Carbohydrate *20 g*; Fat *12 g*; Saturates *6 g*

 very easy

10 mins

40 mins

This robust stew is full of Mediterranean flavours. If you do not want to prepare the fish yourself, ask your local fishmonger to do it for you.

Italian Fish Stew

SERVES 4

2 tbsp olive oil
2 red onions, chopped finely
1 garlic clove, crushed
2 courgettes, sliced
400 g/14 oz canned chopped tomatoes
850 ml/1½ pints fish or vegetable stock
85 g/3 oz dried pasta shapes
350 g/12 oz firm white fish, such as cod, haddock or hake
1 tbsp chopped fresh basil or oregano or 1 tsp dried oregano
1 tsp grated lemon rind
1 tbsp cornflour
1 tbsp water
salt and pepper
fresh basil or oregano sprigs, to garnish

1 Heat the oil in a large pan. Add the onions and garlic and cook over a low heat, stirring occasionally, for about 5 minutes until softened. Add the courgettes and cook, stirring frequently, for 2–3 minutes.

2 Add the tomatoes and stock to the pan and bring to the boil. Add the pasta, bring back to the boil, reduce the heat and cover. Simmer for 5 minutes.

3 Skin and bone the fish, then cut it into chunks. Add to the pan with the basil or oregano and lemon rind and simmer gently for 5 minutes or until the fish is opaque and flakes easily (take care not to overcook it) and the pasta is tender, but still firm to the bite.

4 Blend the cornflour with the water to a smooth paste and stir into the stew. Cook gently for 2 minutes, stirring constantly, until thickened. Season with salt and pepper to taste.

5 Ladle the stew into 4 warmed soup bowls. Garnish with basil or oregano sprigs and serve immediately.

NUTRITION
Calories 236; Sugars 4 g; Protein 20 g;
Carbohydrate 25 g; Fat 7 g; Saturates 1 g

moderate

5–10 mins

25 mins

For the best results, you need to use flavourful fish, such as cod or haddock, for this recipe. Frozen fish fillets are also suitable.

Provençal Fish Soup

1 Heat the oil in a large pan over a medium heat. Add the onions and cook, stirring occasionally, for about 5 minutes until softened. Add the leek, carrot, celery, fennel, if using, and garlic and continue cooking for 4–5 minutes or until the leek is wilted.

2 Add the wine and simmer for 1 minute. Add the tomatoes, bay leaf, fennel seeds, orange rind, saffron and water. Bring just to the boil, reduce the heat, cover and simmer gently, stirring occasionally, for 30 minutes.

3 Add the fish and cook for a further 20–30 minutes or until it flakes easily. Remove the bay leaf and orange rind.

4 Remove the pan from the heat and set aside to cool slightly, then transfer the mixture to a blender or food processor and process to a smooth purée, working in batches if necessary. (If using a food processor, strain off the cooking liquid and reserve. Purée the soup solids with enough cooking liquid to moisten them, then combine with the remaining liquid.)

5 Return the soup to the pan. Taste and adjust the seasoning, if necessary, and simmer for 5–10 minutes or until heated through. Ladle the soup into warmed bowls and sprinkle with croûtons, if using. Serve the soup immediately.

SERVES 4

1 tbsp olive oil
2 onions, chopped finely
1 small leek, sliced thinly
1 small carrot, chopped finely
1 celery stick, chopped finely
1 small fennel bulb, chopped finely (optional)
3 garlic cloves, chopped finely
225 ml/8 fl oz dry white wine
400 g/14 oz canned tomatoes
1 bay leaf
pinch of fennel seeds
2 strips of orange rind
¼ tsp saffron threads
1.2 litres/2 pints water
350 g/12 oz white fish fillets, skinned
salt and pepper
croûtons, to serve (optional)

NUTRITION
Calories *122*; Sugars *6 g*; Protein *12 g*; Carbohydrate *7 g*; Fat *3 g*; Saturates *0 g*

  moderate

10 mins

1 hr 30 mins

The delicate colour of this soup belies its heady flavours. The recipe has been adapted from a French soup thickened with a garlicky mayonnaise.

Garlic Fish Soup

SERVES 4

2 tsp olive oil
1 large onion, chopped
1 small fennel bulb, chopped
1 leek, sliced
3–4 large garlic cloves, sliced thinly
125 ml/4 fl oz dry white wine
1.2 litres/2 pints fish stock
4 tbsp white rice
1 strip lemon rind
1 bay leaf
450 g/1 lb skinless white fish fillets, cut into 4-cm/1½-inch pieces
50 ml/2 fl oz double cream
2 tbsp chopped fresh parsley
salt and pepper

1 Heat the oil in a large saucepan over a medium-low heat. Add the onion, fennel, leek and garlic and cook for 4–5 minutes, stirring frequently, until the onion is softened.

2 Add the wine and bubble briefly. Add the fish stock, rice, lemon rind and bay leaf. Bring the mixture to the boil, reduce the heat to medium-low and simmer for 20–25 minutes or until the rice and vegetables are soft. Remove the lemon rind and bay leaf from the pan.

3 Let the soup cool slightly, then transfer to a blender or a food processor and purée until smooth, working in batches if necessary. (If using a food processor, strain off the cooking liquid and reserve. Purée the soup solids with enough cooking liquid to moisten them, then combine with the remaining liquid.)

4 Return the puréed soup to the saucepan and bring to a simmer. Add the fish pieces to the soup, cover and continue simmering over a low heat, stirring occasionally, for 4–5 minutes or until the fish is cooked and begins to flake. Stir in the cream. Taste and adjust the seasoning, adding salt, if needed, and pepper. Ladle into warmed soup bowls and serve sprinkled with parsley.

NUTRITION

Calories *191*; Sugars *4 g*; Protein *19 g*; Carbohydrate *12 g*; Fat *7 g*; Saturates *3 g*

  easy

5 mins

40–45 mins

Fishermen's soups are variable, depending on the season and the catch. Monkfish has a texture like lobster, but tender cod is equally appealing.

Breton Fish Soup *with* Cider

1 Melt the butter in a large saucepan over a medium–low heat. Add the leek and shallots and cook for about 5 minutes, stirring frequently, until they start to soften. Add the cider and bring to the boil.

2 Stir in the stock, potatoes and bay leaf with a large pinch of salt (unless the stock is salty) and bring back to the boil. Reduce the heat, cover the pan and cook the soup gently for 10 minutes.

3 Put the flour in a small bowl and very slowly whisk in a few tablespoons of the milk to make a thick paste. Stir in more milk, if needed, to make a smooth liquid.

4 Adjust the heat so that the soup bubbles gently. Stir in the flour mixture and cook, stirring frequently, for 5 minutes. Add the remaining milk and half the cream. Continue cooking for about 10 minutes or until the potatoes are tender.

5 Chop the sorrel finely and combine with the remaining cream. (If using a food processor, add the sorrel and chop, then add the cream and process briefly.)

6 Stir the sorrel cream into the soup and add the fish. Continue cooking, stirring occasionally, for about 3 minutes or until the monkfish stiffens or the cod just begins to flake. Taste the soup and adjust the seasoning, if necessary. Ladle into warmed bowls and serve.

SERVES 4

10 g/⅓ oz butter
1 large leek, sliced thinly
2 shallots, chopped finely
300ml/10 fl oz cider
125 ml/4 fl oz fish stock
250 g/9 oz potatoes, diced
1 bay leaf
4 tbsp plain flour
175 ml/6 fl oz milk
175 ml/6 fl oz double cream
55 g/2 oz fresh sorrel leaves
350 g/12 oz skinless monkfish or cod fillet, cut into 2.5-cm/1-inch pieces
salt and pepper

NUTRITION
Calories *103*; Sugars *1.5 g*; Protein *5.2 g*; Carbohydrate *6.6 g*; Fat *6 g*; Saturates *3.8 g*

★★★   moderate

    5–10 mins

    40 mins

This soup can be made in stages, so it is ideal for entertaining because some of it can be prepared in advance.

Mussel *and* Potato Soup

SERVES 4

1 kg/2 lb 4 oz mussels
300 g/10½ oz potatoes
3 tbsp plain flour
600 ml/1 pint milk
300 ml/10 fl oz whipping cream
1–2 garlic cloves, chopped finely
1 large bunch curly parsley leaves
salt and pepper

NUTRITION

Calories 95; Sugars 2 g; Protein 4 g; Carbohydrate 6 g; Fat 6 g; Saturates 4 g

 easy

15 mins

45 mins

1 Discard any broken mussels and open shells that do not close when tapped. Rinse, pull off any 'beards' and scrape off barnacles. Put the mussels in a large heavy-based saucepan. Cover tightly and cook over a high heat for about 4 minutes or until the mussels are open.

2 Remove the mussels from the shells, adding any additional juices to the pan. Strain the cooking liquid through a muslin-lined sieve and set aside.

3 Boil the potatoes, in their skins, in salted water for about 15 minutes or until tender. When cool enough to handle, peel and cut into small cubes.

4 Mix the flour with a few tablespoons of the milk to make a smooth liquid.

5 Put the remaining milk, cream and garlic in a saucepan and bring to the boil. Whisk in the flour mixture. Reduce the heat to medium-low and simmer for about 15 minutes or until the liquid has thickened slightly. Add the parsley and cook for about 2–3 minutes or until bright green and wilted.

6 Allow the soup base to cool slightly, then transfer to a blender or food processor and purée until smooth, working in batches if necessary.

7 Return the purée to the saucepan and stir in the mussel cooking liquid and the potatoes. Season to taste with salt, if needed, and pepper. Simmer the soup gently for 5–7 minutes. Add the mussels and continue cooking for about 2 minutes until the soup is steaming and the mussels are hot. Ladle the soup into warmed bowls and serve.

This colourful mixed seafood soup would be superbly complemented by a dry white wine.

Italian Fish Soup

1 Melt the butter in a large saucepan, add the fish fillets, seafood, crabmeat and onion and cook gently over a low heat for 6 minutes.

2 Add the flour to the mixture, stirring thoroughly to avoid any lumps.

3 Gradually add the fish stock, stirring constantly, until the soup comes to the boil. Reduce the heat and simmer for 30 minutes.

4 Add the pasta to the pan and cook for a further 10 minutes.

5 Stir in the anchovy essence, orange rind, orange juice, sherry and double cream. Season to taste with salt and pepper.

6 Heat the soup until completely warmed through. Transfer the soup to a tureen or to warmed soup bowls and serve with crusty brown bread.

SERVES 4

60 g/2 oz butter
450 g/1 lb assorted fish fillets, such as red mullet and snapper
450 g/1 lb prepared seafood, such as squid and prawns
225 g/8 oz fresh crabmeat
1 large onion, sliced
25 g/1 oz plain flour
1.2 litres/2 pints fish stock
100 g/3½ oz dried pasta shapes, such as ditalini or elbow macaroni
1 tbsp anchovy essence
grated rind and juice of 1 orange
50 ml/2 fl oz dry sherry
300 ml/10 fl oz double cream
salt and black pepper
crusty brown bread, to serve

NUTRITION
Calories *668*; Sugars *3 g*; Protein *48 g*; Carbohydrate *21 g*; Fat *43 g*; Saturates *25 g*

⚜ **COOK'S TIP**

The heads, tails, trimmings and bones of virtually any non-oily fish can be used to make fish stock.

★★★ moderate

5 mins

55 mins

Wild mushrooms are available commercially and an increasing range of cultivated varieties is now to be found in many supermarkets.

Veal *and* Wild Mushroom Soup

SERVES 4

450 g/1 lb veal, sliced thinly
450 g/1 lb veal bones
1.2 litres/2 pints water
1 small onion
6 peppercorns
1 tsp cloves
pinch of mace
140 g/5 oz oyster and shiitake mushrooms, chopped roughly
150 ml/5 fl oz double cream
100 g/3 ½ oz dried vermicelli
1 tbsp cornflour
3 tbsp milk
salt and pepper

1 Put the veal, bones and water into a large saucepan. Bring to the boil and reduce the heat. Add the onion, peppercorns, cloves and mace and simmer for about 3 hours or until the veal stock is reduced by one-third.

2 Strain the stock, skim off any fat on the surface with a slotted spoon and pour the stock into a clean saucepan. Add the veal meat to the pan.

3 Add the mushrooms and cream, bring to the boil over a low heat, then leave to simmer for 12 minutes, stirring occasionally.

4 Meanwhile, cook the vermicelli in lightly salted boiling water for 10 minutes or until tender, but still firm to the bite. Drain and keep warm.

5 Mix the cornflour and milk to form a smooth paste. Stir into the soup to thicken. Season to taste with salt and pepper and just before serving, add the vermicelli. Transfer the soup to a warm tureen and serve immediately.

NUTRITION

Calories *413*; Sugars *3 g*; Protein *28 g*;
Carbohydrate *28 g*; Fat *22 g*; Saturates *12 g*

 moderate

5 mins

3 hrs 15 mins

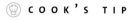 **COOK'S TIP**

You can make this soup with the more inexpensive cuts of veal, such as breast or neck slices. These are lean and the long cooking time ensures that the meat is really tender.

Veal and ham is a classic combination, complemented here with the addition of sherry to create a richly-flavoured Italian soup.

Veal *and* Ham Soup

1 Melt the butter in a large pan. Add the onions, carrot, celery, veal and ham and cook over a low heat for 6 minutes.

2 Sprinkle over the flour and cook, stirring constantly, for a further 2 minutes. Gradually stir in the stock, then add the bay leaf, peppercorns and salt. Bring to the boil and simmer for 1 hour.

3 Remove the pan from the heat and add the redcurrant jelly and cream sherry, stirring to combine. Set aside for about 4 hours.

4 Remove the bay leaf from the pan and discard. Reheat the soup over a very low heat until warmed through.

5 Meanwhile, cook the vermicelli in a saucepan of lightly salted boiling water for 10–12 minutes. Stir the vermicelli into the soup and transfer to soup bowls. Garnish with garlic croûtons.

SERVES 4

60 g/2 oz butter
1 onion, diced
1 carrot, diced
1 celery stick, diced
450 g/1 lb veal, sliced very thinly
450 g/1 lb ham, sliced thinly
60 g/2 oz plain flour
1 litre/1 ¾ pints beef stock
1 bay leaf
8 black peppercorns
pinch of salt
3 tbsp redcurrant jelly
150 ml/5 fl oz cream sherry
100 g/3 ½ oz dried vermicelli
garlic croûtons (see Cook's Tip), to garnish

NUTRITION
Calories *501*; Sugars *10 g*; Protein *38 g*; Carbohydrate *28 g*; Fat *18 g*; Saturates *10 g*

⭐⭐⭐ moderate
🕐 4 hrs 5 mins
🕐 3 hrs 15 mins

 COOK'S TIP

To make garlic croûtons, cut 3 slices of day-old crustless white bread into small cubes. Stir-fry 1–2 chopped garlic cloves in 3 tablspoons of oil for 1–2 minutes. Remove the garlic and cook the bread, stirring, until golden. Remove and drain.

This hearty and nourishing soup, combining chick peas and chicken, is an ideal starter for a family supper.

Chicken *and* Bean Soup

SERVES 4

25 g/1 oz butter
3 spring onions, chopped
2 garlic cloves, crushed
1 fresh marjoram sprig, chopped finely
350 g/12 oz boned chicken breasts, diced
1.2 litres/2 pints chicken stock
350 g/12 oz canned chick peas, drained
1 bouquet garni
1 red pepper, diced
1 green pepper, diced
115 g/4 oz small dried pasta shapes, such as elbow macaroni
salt and white pepper
croûtons, to garnish

1 Melt the butter in a large saucepan. Add the spring onions, garlic, sprig of fresh marjoram and the diced chicken and cook, stirring frequently, over a medium heat for 5 minutes.

2 Add the chicken stock, chick peas and bouquet garni and season with salt and white pepper.

3 Bring the soup to the boil, reduce the heat and simmer for about 2 hours.

4 Add the diced peppers and pasta to the pan, then simmer for a further 20 minutes.

5 Transfer the soup to a warm tureen. To serve, ladle the soup into individual serving bowls and serve immediately, garnished with the croûtons.

NUTRITION

Calories *347*; Sugars *2 g*; Protein *28 g*; Carbohydrate *37 g*; Fat *11 g*; Saturates *4 g*

 moderate

5 mins

2 hrs 30 mins

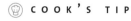 **COOK'S TIP**

If you prefer, you can use dried chick peas. Cover with cold water and set aside to soak for 5–8 hours. Drain and add the beans to the soup, according to the recipe, and allow an additional 30 minutes to 1 hour cooking time.

This delicately flavoured summer soup is surprisingly easy to make, and tastes delicious.

Lemon *and* Chicken Soup

1 Melt the butter in a large saucepan. Add the shallots, carrots, celery and chicken and cook over a low heat, stirring occasionally, for 8 minutes.

2 Thinly pare the lemons and blanch the lemon rind in boiling water for 3 minutes. Squeeze the juice from the lemons.

3 Add the lemon rind and juice to the pan, together with the chicken stock. Bring slowly to the boil over a low heat and simmer for 40 minutes, stirring occasionally. Remove the lemon rind with a slotted spoon.

4 Add the spaghetti to the pan and cook for 15 minutes. Season to taste with salt and white pepper and add the cream. Heat through, but do not allow the soup to boil or it will curdle.

5 Pour the soup into a tureen or individual bowls, garnish with parsley and slices of lemon and serve immediately.

SERVES 4

60 g/2 oz butter
8 shallots, sliced thinly
2 carrots, sliced thinly
2 celery sticks, sliced thinly
225 g/8 oz boned chicken breasts, chopped finely
3 lemons
1.2 litres/2 pints chicken stock
225 g/8 oz dried spaghetti, broken into small pieces
150 ml/5 fl oz double cream
salt and white pepper

to garnish
fresh parsley sprigs
4 lemon slices, halved

NUTRITION
Calories *506*; Sugars *4 g*; Protein *19 g*; Carbohydrate *41 g*; Fat *31 g*; Saturates *19 g*

 moderate

5–10 mins

1 hr 15 mins

 COOK'S TIP

You can prepare this soup up to the end of step 3 in advance, so that all you need do before serving is heat it through before adding and cooking the pasta and the finishing touches.

This aromatic dish originates from Hungary, where goulash soups are often served with dumplings. Noodles are a tasty and quick alternative.

Beef Goulash Soup

SERVES 6

1 tbsp oil
500 g/1 lb 2 oz lean minced beef
2 onions, chopped finely
2 garlic cloves, chopped finely
2 tbsp plain flour
225 ml/8 fl oz water
400 g/14 oz canned chopped tomatoes in juice
1 carrot, chopped finely
225 g/8 oz red pepper, roasted, peeled, deseeded and chopped
1 tsp Hungarian paprika
1/4 tsp caraway seeds
pinch of dried oregano
1 litre/1 3/4 pints beef stock
60 g/2 oz tagliatelle, broken into small pieces
salt and pepper
soured cream and coriander, to garnish

1 Heat the oil in a large wide saucepan over a medium-high heat. Add the beef and sprinkle with salt and pepper. Fry until lightly browned.

2 Reduce the heat and add the onions and garlic. Cook for about 3 minutes, stirring frequently, until the onions are softened. Stir in the flour and continue cooking for 1 minute.

3 Add the water and stir to combine well, scraping the bottom of the pan to mix in the flour. Stir in the tomatoes, carrot, pepper, paprika, caraway seeds, oregano and stock.

4 Bring just to the boil. Reduce the heat, cover and simmer gently for about 40 minutes, stirring occasionally, until all the vegetables are tender.

5 Add the tagliatelle to the soup and simmer for a further 20 minutes or until the tagliatelle are cooked.

6 Taste the soup and adjust the seasoning, if necessary. Ladle into warmed bowls and top each with a tablespoonful of cream. Garnish with coriander.

NUTRITION

Calories 320; Sugars 10 g; Protein 27 g;
Carbohydrate 27 g; Fat 13 g; Saturates 5 g

easy

15 mins

1 hr 15 mins

This soup is full of interesting flavours. The chorizo gives it appealing spicy undertones that marry well with the meaty squid.

Squid, Chorizo *and* Tomato Soup

1 Cut off the squid tentacles and cut into bite-sized pieces. Slice the bodies into rings.

2 Place a large saucepan over a medium-low heat and add the chorizo. Cook for 5–10 minutes, stirring frequently, until it renders most of its fat. Remove with a slotted spoon and drain on paper towels.

3 Pour off all the fat from the pan and add the onion, celery, carrot and garlic. Cover and cook for 3–4 minutes or until the onion is slightly softened.

4 Stir in the tomatoes, fish stock, cumin, saffron, bay leaf and chorizo.

5 Add the squid to the soup. Bring almost to the boil, reduce the heat, cover and cook gently for 40–45 minutes or until the squid and carrot are tender, stirring occasionally.

6 Taste the soup and stir in a little chilli purée for a spicier flavour, if wished. Season with salt and pepper. Ladle into warmed bowls, sprinkle with parsley and serve.

SERVES 6

450 g/1 lb cleaned squid
150 g/5 ½ oz lean chorizo, peeled and diced very finely
1 onion, chopped finely
1 celery stick, sliced thinly
1 carrot, sliced thinly
2 garlic cloves, chopped finely or crushed
400 g/14 oz canned chopped tomatoes in juice
1.2 litres/2 pints fish stock
½ tsp ground cumin
pinch of saffron powder or threads
1 bay leaf
salt and pepper
chilli purée (optional)
fresh parsley sprigs, to garnish

NUTRITION
Calories *165*; Sugars *5 g*; Protein *18 g*; Carbohydrate *7 g*; Fat *8 g*; Saturates *3 g*

★★★   moderate

    15 mins

1 hr

🍳 **COOK'S TIP**

Chorizo varies in the amount of fat and the degree of spiciness. A lean style is best for this soup.

This is a really hearty soup, filled with colour, flavour and goodness, which may be adapted to any vegetables that you have at hand.

Mixed Bean Soup

SERVES 4

1 tbsp vegetable oil

1 red onion, halved and sliced

100 g/3½ oz potato, diced

1 carrot, diced

1 leek, sliced

1 fresh green chilli, sliced

3 garlic cloves, crushed

1 tsp ground coriander

1 tsp chilli powder

1 litre/1¾ pints vegetable stock

450 g/1 lb mixed canned beans, such as red kidney, borlotti, black eye or flageolet, drained and rinsed

salt and pepper

2 tbsp chopped fresh coriander, to garnish

1 Heat the oil in a large pan and add the onion, potato, carrot and leek. Cook, stirring occasionally, for 2 minutes or until the vegetables are slightly softened.

2 Add the fresh chilli and garlic and cook for 1 further minute.

3 Stir in the ground coriander, chilli powder and the vegetable stock.

4 Bring the soup to the boil, reduce the heat and cook for 20 minutes or until the vegetables are tender.

5 Stir in the beans, season to taste and cook, stirring occasionally, for a further 10 minutes.

6 Ladle the soup into bowls, garnish with chopped coriander and serve.

NUTRITION

Calories *190*; Sugars *9 g*; Protein *10 g*; Carbohydrate *30 g*; Fat *4 g*; Saturates *0.5 g*

 very easy

5 mins

40 mins

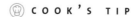 **COOK'S TIP**

Serve this soup with slices of warm corn bread or a cheese loaf.

This wonderful combination of cannellini beans, vegetables and vermicelli is made even richer by the addition of pesto and dried mushrooms.

Vegetable *and* Bean Soup

1 Slice the aubergine into rings about 1 cm/½ inch thick, then cut each ring into quarters.

2 Cut the tomatoes and potato into small dice. Cut the carrot into sticks, about 2.5 cm/1 inch long and cut the leek into rings.

3 Place the cannellini beans and their liquid in a large saucepan. Add the aubergine, tomatoes, potatoes, carrot and leek, stirring to mix.

4 Add the stock to the pan and bring to the boil. Reduce the heat and leave to simmer for 15 minutes.

5 Add the basil, dried mushrooms and their soaking liquid and the vermicelli and simmer for 5 minutes or until all of the vegetables are tender.

6 Remove the pan from the heat and stir in the pesto.

7 Serve with freshly grated Parmesan cheese, if using.

SERVES 4

1 small aubergine
2 large tomatoes
1 potato, peeled
1 carrot, peeled
1 leek
425 g/15 oz canned cannellini beans
850 ml/1½ pints hot vegetable or
    chicken stock
2 tsp dried basil
15 g/ ½ oz dried porcini mushrooms,
    soaked for 10 minutes in enough warm
    water to cover
50 g/1 ¾ oz vermicelli
3 tbsp pesto (see page 77 or use
    shop bought)
freshly grated Parmesan cheese, to serve
    (optional)

NUTRITION
Calories *294*; Sugars *2 g*; Protein *11 g*;
Carbohydrate *30 g*; Fat *16 g*; Saturates *2 g*

⭐⭐   easy

🖐   30 mins

     30 mins

A thick vegetable soup which is a delicious meal in itself. Serve with Parmesan cheese and warm sun-dried tomato-flavoured ciabatta bread.

Chick Pea Soup

SERVES 4

2 tbsp olive oil
2 leeks, sliced
2 courgettes, diced
2 garlic cloves, crushed
800 g/28 oz canned chopped tomatoes
1 tbsp tomato purée
1 fresh bay leaf
850 ml/1 ½ pints chicken stock
400 g/14 oz canned chick peas,
    drained and rinsed
225 g/8 oz spinach
salt and pepper

to serve
freshly grated Parmesan cheese
sun-dried tomato bread

1 Heat the oil in a large saucepan, add the leeks and courgettes and cook briskly for 5 minutes, stirring constantly.

2 Add the garlic, tomatoes, tomato purée, bay leaf, stock and chick peas. Bring to the boil and simmer for 5 minutes.

3 Shred the spinach finely, add to the soup and cook for 2 minutes. Season.

4 Remove the bay leaf from the soup and discard.

5 Serve the soup with freshly grated Parmesan cheese and sun-dried tomato bread.

NUTRITION
Calories *297*; Sugars *0 g*; Protein *11 g*;
Carbohydrate *24 g*; Fat *18 g*; Saturates *2 g*

 very easy

 5 mins

15 mins

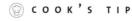 **COOK'S TIP**

Chick peas are used extensively in North African cuisine and are also found in Italian, Spanish, Middle Eastern and Indian cooking. They have a deliciously nutty flavour with a firm texture and are an excellent canned product.

Beans feature widely in Italian soups, making them hearty and tasty. The beans need to be soaked overnight, so prepare well in advance.

Red Bean Soup

1 Drain the beans and place them in a saucepan with enough fresh water to cover. Bring to the boil, then boil for 15 minutes to remove any harmful toxins. Reduce the heat and simmer for 45 minutes.

2 Drain the beans and put into a clean saucepan with the water, ham bone or knuckle, carrots, onion, celery, leek, bay leaves and olive oil. Bring to the boil, then cover and simmer for 1 hour or until the beans are very tender.

3 Discard the bay leaves and bone, reserving any ham pieces from the bone. Remove a small cupful of the beans and reserve. Purée or liquidize the soup in a food processor or blender, or push through a coarse sieve, and return to a clean pan.

4 Add the tomatoes, garlic, tomato purée, rice and season with salt and pepper. Bring back to the boil and simmer for about 15 minutes or until the rice is tender.

5 Add the cabbage and reserved beans and ham and continue to simmer for 5 minutes. Adjust the seasoning and serve very hot. If liked, a piece of toasted crusty bread may be put in the base of each soup bowl before ladling in the soup. If the soup is too thick, add a little boiling water or stock.

SERVES 4

175 g/6 oz dried red kidney beans, soaked overnight
1.7 litres/3 pints water
1 large ham bone or bacon knuckle
2 carrots, chopped
1 large onion, chopped
2 celery sticks, sliced thinly
1 leek, trimmed, washed and sliced
1–2 bay leaves
2 tbsp olive oil
2–3 tomatoes, peeled and chopped
1 garlic clove, crushed
1 tbsp tomato purée
60 g/2 oz arborio or Italian rice
115–175 g/4–6 oz green cabbage, shredded finely
salt and pepper

NUTRITION

Calories *184*; Sugars *5 g*; Protein *4 g*; Carbohydrate *19 g*; Fat *11 g*; Saturates *2 g*

 easy

 5–10 mins

5 hrs 45 mins

In Italy, this soup is called Minestrade Lentiche. A minestra is a soup cooked with pasta; here, farfalline, a small bow-shaped variety, is used.

Brown Lentil *and* Pasta Soup

SERVES 4

4 rashers streaky bacon, cut into small squares
1 onion, chopped
2 garlic cloves, crushed
2 celery sticks, chopped
50 g/1¾ oz farfalline or spaghetti, broken into small pieces
400 g/14 oz canned brown lentils, drained
1.2 litres/2 pints hot ham or vegetable stock
2 tbsp chopped fresh mint

1 Place the bacon in a large frying pan together with the onion, garlic and celery. Cook for 4–5 minutes, stirring, until the onion is tender and the bacon is just beginning to brown.

2 Add the pasta to the pan and cook, stirring, for about 1 minute to coat the pasta in the oil.

3 Add the lentils and the stock and bring to the boil. Reduce the heat and leave to simmer for 12–15 minutes or until the pasta is tender.

4 Remove the pan from the heat and stir in the chopped fresh mint.

5 Transfer the soup to warmed soup bowls and serve immediately.

NUTRITION

Calories *225*; Sugars *1 g*; Protein *13 g*;
Carbohydrate *27 g*; Fat *8 g*; Saturates *3 g*

 very easy

5 mins

25 mins

👨‍🍳 COOK'S TIP

If you prefer to use dried lentils, add the stock before the pasta and cook for 1–1¼ hours or until the lentils are tender. Add the pasta and cook for a further 12–15 minutes.

Minestrone translates as 'big soup' in Italian. It is made all over Italy, but this version comes from Livorno, a port on the western coast.

Minestrone

1 Heat the olive oil in a large saucepan. Add the diced pancetta, chopped onions and garlic and fry, stirring, for about 5 minutes or until the onions are soft and golden.

2 Add the prepared potato, carrot, leek, cabbage and celery to the saucepan. Cook for a further 2 minutes, stirring frequently, to coat all of the vegetables in the oil.

3 Add the tomatoes, flageolet beans, hot ham or chicken stock and bouquet garni to the pan, stirring to mix. Leave the soup to simmer, covered, for 15–20 minutes or until all of the vegetables are just tender.

4 Remove the bouquet garni, season with salt and pepper to taste and serve with plenty of freshly grated Parmesan cheese.

SERVES 4

1 tbsp olive oil
100 g/3½ oz pancetta ham, diced
2 medium onions, chopped
2 garlic cloves , crushed
1 potato, peeled and cut into
   1-cm/½-inch cubes
1 carrot, peeled and cut into chunks
1 leek, sliced into rings
¼ green cabbage, shredded
1 celery stick, chopped
450 g/1 lb canned chopped tomatoes
200 g/7 oz canned flageolet beans, drained
   and rinsed
600 ml/1 pint hot ham or chicken stock,
   diluted with 600 ml/1 pint boiling water
bouquet garni (2 bay leaves, 2 rosemary
   sprigs and 2 thyme sprigs, tied together)
salt and pepper
freshly grated Parmesan cheese, to serve

NUTRITION
Calories 311; Sugars 8 g; Protein 12 g;
Carbohydrate 26 g; Fat 19 g; Saturates 5 g

⭐ very easy
🖐 10 mins
🕐 30 mins

This classic soup is very popular throughout the world. When pumpkin is out of season, use butternut squash in its place.

Pumpkin Soup

SERVES 6

about 1 kg/2 lb 4 oz pumpkin
40 g/1½ oz butter or margarine
1 onion, sliced thinly
1 garlic clove, crushed
900 ml/1½ pints vegetable stock
½ tsp ground ginger
1 tbsp lemon juice
3–4 thinly pared strips of
 orange rind (optional)
1–2 bay leaves or 1 bouquet garni
300 ml/10 fl oz milk
salt and pepper

to garnish
4–6 tablespoons single or double cream,
 natural yogurt or fromage frais
snipped chives

1 Peel the pumpkin, remove the seeds, then cut the flesh into 2.5-cm/1-inch cubes.

2 Melt the butter or margarine in a large, heavy-based saucepan. Add the onion and garlic and cook over a low heat until soft but not coloured.

3 Add the pumpkin and toss with the onion for 2–3 minutes.

4 Add the stock and bring to the boil over a medium heat. Season to taste with salt and pepper and add the ground ginger and lemon juice, the strips of orange rind, if using, and the bay leaves or bouquet garni.

5 Cover the pan and gently simmer the soup over a low heat for about 20 minutes, stirring occasionally, until the pumpkin is tender.

6 Discard the orange rind, if using, and the bay leaves or bouquet garni. Cool the soup slightly, then press through a sieve with the back of a spoon, or process in a food processor until smooth. Pour into a clean saucepan.

7 Add the milk and reheat gently. Adjust the seasoning. Garnish with a swirl of cream, natural yogurt or fromage frais and snipped chives, then serve.

NUTRITION
Calories *112*; Sugars *7 g*; Protein *4 g*;
Carbohydrate *8 g*; Fat *7 g*; Saturates *2 g*

 very easy

 10 mins

30 mins

Sweet red peppers and tangy tomatoes are blended together in a smooth vegetable soup that makes a perfect starter or light lunch.

Tomato *and* Red Pepper Soup

1 Preheat the grill to hot. Halve and deseed the peppers, arrange them on the grill rack and cook, turning occasionally, for 8–10 minutes or until softened and charred.

2 Leave to cool slightly, then carefully peel off the charred skin. Reserving a small piece for garnish, chop the pepper flesh and place in a large saucepan.

3 Mix in the onion, celery and garlic. Add the stock and the bay leaves. Bring to the boil, cover and simmer for 15 minutes. Remove from the heat.

4 Stir in the tomatoes and transfer to a blender. Process for a few seconds until smooth. Return to the saucepan.

5 Season to taste and heat for 3–4 minutes or until piping hot. Ladle into warmed bowls and garnish with the reserved pepper cut into strips and the spring onion floating on the top. Serve with crusty bread.

SERVES 4

2 large red peppers
1 large onion, chopped
2 celery sticks, trimmed and chopped
1 garlic clove, crushed
600 ml/1 pint vegetable stock
2 bay leaves
800 g/28 oz canned plum tomatoes
salt and pepper
2 spring onions, shredded finely, to garnish
crusty bread, to serve

NUTRITION
Calories *52*; Sugars *9 g*; Protein *3 g*;
Carbohydrate *10 g*; Fat *0.4 g*; Saturates *0 g*

 moderate

 1 hr 15 mins

 35 mins

COOK'S TIP

If you prefer a coarser, more robust soup, lightly mash the tomatoes with a wooden spoon and omit the blending process in step 4.

This delicately flavoured apple and apricot soup is gently spiced with ginger and allspice and finished with a swirl of soured cream.

Spiced Fruit Soup

SERVES 4

125 g/4½ oz dried apricots, soaked overnight, or no-need-to-soak dried apricots
500 g/1 lb 2 oz eating apples, peeled, cored and chopped
1 small onion, chopped
1 tbsp lemon or lime juice
700 ml/1¼ pints vegetable stock
150 ml/5 fl oz dry white wine
¼ tsp ground ginger
pinch of ground allspice
salt and pepper

to garnish
4–6 tbsp soured cream
ground ginger or ground allspice

1 Drain the apricots, if necessary, and chop coarsely.

2 Put the apricots in a pan and add the apples, onion, lemon or lime juice and stock. Bring to the boil, cover and simmer gently for about 20 minutes or until the apples and onions are tender.

3 Set the soup aside to cool a little, then press through a sieve or process in a food processor or blender until a smooth purée is formed. Pour the fruit soup into a clean pan.

4 Add the wine and spices and season to taste. Bring back to the boil, then set aside to cool. If it is too thick, add a little more stock or water, then chill in the refrigerator for several hours.

5 Garnish with soured cream and dust lightly with ginger or allspice.

NUTRITION
Calories *147*; Sugars *28 g*; Protein *3 g*;
Carbohydrate *29 g*; Fat *0.4 g*; Saturates *0 g*

⊛⊛ easy

 7 hrs 45 mins

🕐 25 mins

🍴 **COOK'S TIP**

Other fruits can be combined with apples to make fruit soups – try raspberries, blackberries, blackcurrants or cherries. If the fruits have a lot of pips or stones, sieve the soup after puréeing.

Spinach is the basis for this delicious soup, which has creamy mascarpone cheese stirred through it to give it a wonderful texture.

Spinach *and* Mascarpone Soup

1 Melt half the butter in a very large saucepan. Add the spring onions and celery, and cook them over a medium heat, stirring frequently, for about 5 minutes or until softened.

2 Pack the spinach, sorrel or watercress into the saucepan. Add the stock and bring to the boil, then reduce the heat, cover and simmer for 5–10 minutes.

3 Transfer the soup to a blender or food processor and process until smooth. Alternatively, rub it through a sieve. Return to the saucepan.

4 Add the mascarpone to the soup and heat gently, stirring constantly, until smooth and blended. Season to taste with salt and pepper.

5 Heat the remaining butter with the oil in a frying pan. Add the bread cubes and fry, turning frequently, until golden brown, adding the caraway seeds towards the end of cooking, so that they do not burn.

6 Ladle the soup into warmed bowls. Sprinkle with the croûtons and serve with the sesame bread sticks.

SERVES 4

60 g/2 oz butter
1 bunch spring onions, trimmed and chopped
2 celery sticks, chopped
350 g/12 oz spinach or sorrel, or 3 bunches watercress
850 ml /1½ pints vegetable stock
225 g/8 oz mascarpone cheese
1 tbsp olive oil
2 slices thick-cut bread, cut into cubes
½ tsp caraway seeds
salt and pepper
sesame bread sticks, to serve

NUTRITION
Calories *402*; Sugars *2 g*; Protein *11 g*; Carbohydrate *10 g*; Fat *36 g*; Saturates *21 g*

 very easy
 15 mins
🕐 30 mins

👨‍🍳 COOK'S TIP

Any leafy vegetable can be used to vary the flavour of this soup. For anyone who grows their own vegetables, it is the perfect recipe for experimenting with a glut of produce. Try young beetroot leaves or surplus lettuces.

International Soups

Today people travel the world as a matter of course, and as we have access to more culinary influences our tastes have become more demanding. This chapter caters for that desire for unusual recipes by featuring an international range of modern-day soups, incorporating unusual ingredients such as sweet potato and rocket and flavourings like curry and dill. Recipes have been drawn from Senegal, Eastern Europe, the Americas and the Caribbean; there is something for the most discerning of palates to enjoy.

When there's a chill in the air, this vivid soup is just the thing to serve – it's very warm and comforting.

Sweet Potato Soup

SERVES 6

350 g/12 oz sweet potatoes
1 acorn squash
4 shallots
olive oil
5–6 garlic cloves, unpeeled
850 ml/1½ pints vegetable stock
125 ml/4 fl oz single cream
salt and pepper
snipped chives, to garnish

NUTRITION
Calories 57; Sugars 1.5 g; Protein 2.3 g;
Carbohydrate 6.6 g; Fat 2.5 g; Saturates 1 g

  moderate

15 mins

1 hr 15 mins

1 Cut the sweet potatoes, squash and shallots in half lengthways. Brush the cut sides with oil.

2 Put the vegetables, cut sides down, in a shallow roasting tin. Add the garlic cloves. Roast in a preheated oven at 190°C/375°F/Gas Mark 5 for about 40 minutes or until tender and light brown.

3 When cool, scoop the flesh from the potato and squash halves and put in a saucepan with the shallots. Remove the garlic peel and add the soft insides to the other vegetables.

4 Add the stock and a pinch of salt. Bring just to the boil, reduce the heat and simmer, partially covered, for about 30 minutes, stirring occasionally, until the vegetables are very tender.

5 Allow the soup to cool slightly, then transfer to a blender or food processor and purée until smooth, working in batches, if necessary. (If using a food processor, strain off the cooking liquid and reserve. Purée the soup solids with enough cooking liquid to moisten them, then combine with the remaining liquid.)

6 Return the soup to the saucepan and stir in most of the cream. Season to taste, then simmer for 5–10 minutes or until completely heated through. Ladle into warmed bowls and serve with a swirl of the remaining cream and garnished with snipped chives.

A dried ancho chilli adds a kick to this glowing Mexican corn soup. The sweetcorn is tossed in butter, giving the soup a roasted flavour.

Corn Soup *with* Chillies

1 Put the chilli in a bowl and cover with boiling water. Stand for about 15 minutes to soften.

2 Melt the butter in a frying pan over a medium-low heat. Add the sweetcorn and turn to coat thoroughly. Cook for about 15 minutes, stirring frequently, until the corn starts to brown slightly. Add the onion, garlic and pepper and cook for about 7–10 minutes, stirring frequently, until the onion is softened and the mixture starts to stick.

3 Transfer the mixture to a blender or food processor, add the stock and purée until smooth.

4 Put the cream in a large saucepan, stir in the puréed vegetables and bring the mixture almost to the boil. Add the cumin. Season with a little salt. Adjust the heat so the soup bubbles very gently and cook until the mixture is reduced by about one-quarter.

5 Remove the ancho chilli from its liquid and discard the core and the seeds. (Wash hands well after handling chillies.) Put the chilli into a blender or food processor with 4–5 tablespoons of the soaking water and purée until smooth. Stir 2–4 tablespoons of the purée into the soup, according to taste, and continue cooking for a further 5 minutes.

6 Taste the soup and adjust the seasoning, if necessary. Ladle the soup into warmed bowls, garnish with coriander or parsley and serve.

SERVES 4

1 dried ancho chilli
55 g/2 oz butter
500 g/1 lb 2 oz frozen sweetcorn kernels, defrosted
1 large onion, chopped finely
1 large garlic clove, chopped finely
1 red pepper, cored, deseeded and chopped finely
300 ml/10 fl oz vegetable stock or water
600 ml/1 pint whipping cream
½ tsp ground cumin
salt
fresh coriander or parsley, chopped, to garnish

NUTRITION

Calories *824*; Sugars *12 g*; Protein *9 g*; Carbohydrate *33 g*; Fat *74 g*; Saturates *45 g*

⭐⭐⭐ moderate

🕐 25 mins

 30 mins

Glass bowls are pretty for serving this soup, which makes a very light and refreshing starter for a summer lunch.

Melon Gazpacho

SERVES 4

1 tsp oil
1 onion, chopped finely
1 large garlic clove, chopped finely
1 tsp chopped fresh chilli
700 g/1 lb 9 oz seedless Cantaloupe melon flesh, cubed
½ tsp raspberry vinegar or 1 tsp lemon juice
½ ripe green melon, such as Galia (about 500 g/1 lb 2 oz)
salt
chives, to garnish

1 Heat the oil in a small pan over a low heat. Add the onion, garlic and chilli and cook, stirring occasionally, for about 6–7 minutes or until the onion is softened, but not browned.

2 Put the Cantaloupe melon flesh in a blender or food processor, add the onion, garlic and chilli and process to a smooth purée, stopping to scrape down the sides as needed. You may need to work in batches. Add the vinegar or lemon juice with a pinch of salt and process briefly to combine.

3 Cover with clingfilm and chill in the refrigerator for about 30 minutes or until the mixture is cold.

4 Remove the seeds from the green melon, then cut into balls with a melon baller. Alternatively, cut into cubes with a sharp knife.

5 Divide the soup between 4 shallow bowls and top with the green melon balls. Sprinkle lightly with chives to garnish and serve.

NUTRITION
Calories *98*; Sugars *20 g*; Protein *3 g*; Carbohydrate *21 g*; Fat *1 g*; Saturates *0 g*

    easy

    45 mins

    6–7 mins

🍳 **COOK'S TIP**

If you are wary of using fresh chilli, omit it and add a few drops of hot pepper sauce to taste at the end of Step 2 to liven up the soup.

This soup is made from raw vegetables and fruit, so it is full of goodness as well as flavour and is wonderfully refreshing on a warm day.

Cold Tomato *and* Orange Soup

1 Working over a bowl to catch the juices, peel the oranges. Cut down between the membranes and drop the orange segments into the bowl.

2 Put the tomatoes in a small bowl and pour over boiling water to cover. Stand for 10 seconds, then drain. Peel off the skins and cut the tomatoes in half crossways. Scoop out the seeds into a strainer set over a bowl; reserve the tomato juices.

3 Put the tomatoes, celery and carrots in a blender or food processor. Add the orange segments and their juice and the juice saved from the tomatoes. Process to a smooth purée.

4 Scrape into a bowl and stir in the tomato juice. Cover with clingfilm and chill for about 30 minutes or until cold.

5 Taste the soup and add salt, if needed, and a few drops of Tabasco sauce, if wished. Stir in the chopped mint, ladle into cold bowls and garnish with fresh mint sprigs.

SERVES 4

3 large seedless oranges
4 ripe tomatoes
2 celery sticks, chopped
3 carrots, grated
350 ml/12 fl oz tomato juice
salt
Tabasco sauce (optional)
1 tbsp chopped fresh mint
fresh mint sprigs, to garnish

NUTRITION
Calories *98*; Sugars *22 g*; Protein *3 g*; Carbohydrate *22 g*; Fat *00 g*; Saturates *0 g*

 COOK'S TIP

This soup really needs to be made in a blender for the best texture. A food processor can be used, but the soup will not be completely smooth.

easy

45 mins

00 mins

There are innumerable versions of this soup of Eastern European origin. This refreshing vegetarian version is light and flavourful.

Chilled Borscht

SERVES 4

¼ medium cabbage, cored and chopped coarsely
1 tbsp vegetable oil
1 onion, chopped finely
1 leek, halved lengthways and sliced
400 g/14 oz canned peeled tomatoes
1.2 litres/2 pints water, plus extra if needed
1 carrot, sliced thinly
1 small parsnip, chopped finely
3 beetroot (raw or cooked), peeled and cubed
1 bay leaf
350 ml/12 fl oz tomato juice
2–3 tbsp chopped fresh dill
fresh lemon juice, optional
salt and pepper
soured cream or natural yogurt, to garnish

NUTRITION
Calories *93*; Sugars *12 g*; Protein *4 g*;
Carbohydrate *15 g*; Fat *3 g*; Saturates *0 g*

 moderate

45 mins

1 hr 30 mins

1 Cover the cabbage generously with cold water in a pan. Bring to the boil, cook for 3 minutes, then drain.

2 Heat the oil in a large pan over a medium-low heat. Add the onion and leek, cover and cook, stirring occasionally, for about 5 minutes or until the vegetables begin to soften.

3 Add the tomatoes, water, carrot, parsnip, beetroot and bay leaf. Stir in the blanched cabbage and add a pinch of salt. Bring to the boil, reduce the heat and simmer for about 1¼ hours or until all the vegetables are tender. Remove and discard the bay leaf.

4 Remove the pan from the heat and set aside to cool slightly, then transfer to a blender or food processor and process to a smooth purée, working in batches if necessary. (If using a food processor, strain off the cooking liquid and reserve. Purée the soup solids with enough cooking liquid to moisten them, then combine with the remaining liquid.)

5 Scrape the soup into a large container and stir in the tomato juice. Set aside to cool, then chill in the refrigerator.

6 Stir in the dill. Thin the soup with more tomato juice or water, if wished. Season to taste with salt and pepper and lemon juice, if wished. Ladle into chilled soup bowls, top each with a spiral of soured cream or a spoon of yogurt.

A chunky mix of colourful vegetables, highlighted with Mexican flavours, this cold soup makes a lively starter to any meal.

Iced Salsa Soup

1 Cut the corn kernels from the cobs, or if using frozen sweetcorn, thaw and drain.

2 Heat the oil in a pan over a medium-high heat. Add the peppers and cook, stirring briskly, for 3 minutes. Add the onion and continue cooking for about 2 minutes or until it starts to colour slightly.

3 Add the tomatoes, corn and chilli powder. Continue cooking, stirring frequently, for 1 minute. Pour in the water and when it begins to boil, reduce the heat, cover and cook for a further 4–5 minutes or until the peppers are just barely tender.

4 Transfer the mixture to a large container and stir in the tomato juice. Season with salt and pepper to taste and add more chilli powder, if wished. Cover with clingfilm and chill in the refrigerator until cold.

5 Taste and adjust the seasoning. For a spicier soup, stir in a little chilli purée to taste. For a thinner soup, add a small amount of iced water. Ladle into chilled bowls and garnish with spring onions and fresh coriander leaves.

SERVES 4

2 large corn cobs or 225 g/8 oz frozen sweetcorn kernels
1 tbsp olive oil
1 orange or red pepper, deseeded and chopped finely
1 green pepper, deseeded and chopped finely
1 sweet onion, such as Vidalia, chopped finely
3 ripe tomatoes, peeled, deseeded and chopped
½ tsp chilli powder
125 ml/4 fl oz water
450 ml/16 fl oz tomato juice
chilli purée, optional
salt and pepper

to garnish
3–4 spring onions, chopped finely
fresh coriander leaves, chopped

NUTRITION
Calories *138*; Sugars *12 g*; Protein *5 g*; Carbohydrate *22 g*; Fat *4 g*; Saturates *1 g*

⭐⭐ easy
🕐 45 mins
 12–15 mins

This simple recipe uses the sweet potato with its distinctive flavour and colour, combined with a hint of orange and coriander.

Sweet Potato *and* Onion Soup

S E R V E S 4

2 tbsp vegetable oil
900 g/2 lb sweet potatoes, diced
1 carrot, diced
2 onions, sliced
2 garlic cloves, crushed
600 ml/1 pint vegetable stock
300 ml/10 fl oz unsweetened orange juice
225 ml/8 fl oz low-fat natural yogurt
2 tbsp chopped fresh coriander
salt and pepper

to garnish
fresh coriander sprigs
orange rind

1 Heat the vegetable oil in a large, heavy-based saucepan and add the sweet potatoes, carrot, onions and garlic. Sauté the vegetables over a low heat, stirring constantly, for 5 minutes or until they are softened.

2 Pour in the vegetable stock and orange juice and bring to the boil.

3 Reduce the heat to a simmer, cover the saucepan and cook the vegetables for 20 minutes or until the sweet potatoes and carrot are tender.

4 Transfer the mixture to a food processor or blender in batches and process for 1 minute until puréed. Return the purée to the rinsed-out saucepan.

5 Stir in the yogurt and chopped coriander and season to taste with salt and pepper.

6 Serve the soup in warmed bowls and garnish with coriander sprigs and orange rind.

N U T R I T I O N
Calories *320*; Sugars *26 g*; Protein *7 g*; Carbohydrate *62 g*; Fat *7 g*; Saturates *1 g*

 very easy
 15 mins
 30 mins

 C O O K ' S T I P

This soup can be chilled before serving, if preferred. If chilling, stir the yogurt into the dish just before serving. Serve in chilled bowls.

This hearty soup is wonderful made in the middle of winter with fresh seasonal vegetables. Use a really well-flavoured mature Cheddar cheese.

Cheesy Vegetable Chowder

1 Melt the butter in a large heavy-based saucepan over a medium-low heat. Add the onion, leek and garlic. Cover and cook for about 5 minutes, stirring frequently, until the vegetables are starting to soften.

2 Stir the flour into the vegetables and continue cooking for 2 minutes. Add a little of the stock and stir well, scraping the bottom of the pan to mix in the flour. Bring to the boil, stirring frequently, and slowly stir in the rest of the stock.

3 Add the carrots, celery, turnip, potato, thyme and bay leaf. Reduce the heat, cover the pan and cook the soup gently for about 35 minutes, stirring occasionally, until the vegetables are tender. Remove the bay leaf and the thyme sprigs.

4 Stir in the cream and simmer over a very low heat for 5 minutes.

5 Add the cheese a handful at a time, stirring constantly for 1 minute after each addition to make sure it is completely melted. Taste the soup and adjust the seasoning, adding salt if needed, and pepper to taste.

6 Ladle the soup immediately into warmed bowls, sprinkle with chopped fresh parsley and serve.

SERVES 4

25 g/1 oz butter
1 large onion, chopped finely
1 large leek, split lengthways and sliced thinly
1–2 garlic cloves, crushed
55 g/2 oz plain flour
1.2 litres/2 pints vegetable stock
3 carrots, diced finely
2 celery sticks, diced finely
1 turnip, diced finely
1 large potato, diced finely
3–4 fresh thyme sprigs or ⅛ tsp dried thyme
1 bay leaf
350 ml/12 fl oz single cream
300 g/10½ oz mature Cheddar cheese, grated
chopped fresh parsley, to garnish
salt and pepper

NUTRITION
Calories *669*; Sugars *13 g*; Protein *26 g*; Carbohydrate *33 g*; Fat *49 g*; Saturates *30 g*

⭐⭐⭐ moderate
🕐 15 mins
🕐 50 mins

Rocket has a distinctive flavour that blends well with lettuce in this delicious creamy soup. The rice adds body to the soup.

Lettuce *and* Rocket Soup

SERVES 4

15 g/¹⁄₂ oz butter
1 large sweet onion, such as Vidalia, halved and sliced
2 leeks, sliced
1.5 litres/2³⁄₄ pints vegetable stock
85 g/3 oz white rice
2 carrots, sliced thinly
3 garlic cloves
1 bay leaf
2 heads soft round lettuce (about 500 g/ 1 lb 2 oz), cored and chopped
175 ml/6 fl oz double cream
freshly grated nutmeg
85 g/3 oz rocket leaves, chopped finely
salt and pepper
rocket leaves, to garnish

NUTRITION
Calories *253*; Sugars *8 g*; Protein *4 g*; Carbohydrate *21 g*; Fat *18 g*; Saturates *10 g*

moderate

15 mins

55 mins

1 Melt the butter in a large saucepan over a medium heat and add the onion and leeks. Cover and cook for 3–4 minutes, stirring frequently, until the vegetables begin to soften.

2 Add the stock, rice, carrots, garlic and bay leaf with a large pinch of salt. Bring just to the boil. Reduce the heat, cover and simmer for 25–30 minutes, or until the rice and vegetables are tender. Remove the bay leaf.

3 Add the lettuce to the saucepan and cook for 10 minutes or until the leaves are soft, stirring occasionally.

4 Allow the soup to cool slightly, then transfer to a blender or a food processor and purée until smooth, working in batches if necessary. (If using a food processor, strain off the cooking liquid and reserve. Purée the soup solids with enough cooking liquid to moisten them, then combine with the remaining liquid.)

5 Return the soup to the saucepan and place over a medium-low heat. Stir in the cream and a grating of nutmeg. Simmer for about 5 minutes, stirring occasionally, until the soup is reheated. Add more water or cream if you prefer a thinner soup.

6 Add the rocket leaves and simmer for 2–3 minutes, stirring occasionally, until they are wilted. Adjust the seasoning, ladle the soup into warmed bowls and garnish with rocket leaves.

This tasty soup uses canned tuna and tomatoes, two store cupboard favourites that you are likely to have on hand, for a quickly made lunch.

Curried Tuna Chowder

1 Drain the tuna over a measuring jug and add boiling water to make up the liquid to 600 ml/1 pint.

2 Melt the butter in a large saucepan over a medium-low heat. Add the onion and garlic and cook for about 5 minutes or until the onion is softened, stirring frequently.

3 Stir in the flour and curry powder. Continue cooking for 2 minutes.

4 Slowly add about half of the tuna juice and water mixture and stir well, scraping the bottom of the pan to mix in the flour. Pour in the remaining mixture and bring just to the boil, stirring frequently. Add the tomatoes and break up with a spoon. When the soup almost comes back to the boil, stir in the rice, reduce the heat, cover and simmer for about 10 minutes.

5 Add the tuna and courgette to the soup and continue cooking for about 15 minutes or until the vegetables and rice are tender.

6 Stir in the cream, season with salt and pepper to taste and continue simmering for about 3–4 minutes or until heated through. Ladle the soup into warmed bowls, garnish with parsley and cherry tomatoes and serve.

SERVES 4

200 g/7 oz canned light meat tuna packed in water
20 g/3/4 oz butter
1 onion, chopped finely
1 garlic clove, chopped finely
2 tbsp plain flour
2 tsp mild curry powder
400 g/14 oz canned plum tomatoes in juice
3 tbsp white rice
1 courgette, finely diced
125 ml/4 fl oz single cream
salt and pepper

to garnish
flat leaf parsley
4 cherry tomatoes

NUTRITION
Calories *239*; Sugars *5 g*; Protein *16 g*;
Carbohydrate *20 g*; Fat *11 g*; Saturates *7 g*

moderate

5–10 mins

40–50 mins

Mussels, an economical choice at the fishmonger, give essential flavour to this soup. The proportions of fish and prawns are flexible.

Seafood Chowder

SERVES **6**

1 kg/2 lb 4 oz mussels
4 tbsp plain flour
1.5 litres/2¾ pints fish stock
15 g/½ oz butter
1 large onion, chopped finely
350 g/12 oz skinless white fish fillets, such as cod, sole or haddock
200 g/7 oz cooked or raw peeled prawns
300 ml/10 fl oz whipping cream or double cream
salt and pepper

to garnish
fresh dill sprigs
lemon slices

NUTRITION
Calories *449*; Sugars *4 g*; Protein *34 g*;
Carbohydrate *18 g*; Fat *27 g*; Saturates *16 g*

     moderate

                        30 mins

                        40 mins

1 Discard any broken mussels and those with open shells that do not close when tapped. Rinse, pull off any 'beards', and if there are barnacles, scrape them off with a knife under cold running water. Put the mussels in a large, heavy-based saucepan. Cover tightly and cook over a high heat for about 4 minutes or until the mussels open, shaking the pan occasionally. Remove the mussels from their shells, adding any juices to the cooking liquid. Strain this through a muslin-lined sieve and reserve.

2 Put the flour in a mixing bowl and very slowly whisk in enough of the stock to make a thick paste. Whisk in a little more stock to make a smooth liquid.

3 Melt the butter in heavy-based saucepan over a medium-low heat. Add the onion, cover and cook for about 5 minutes, stirring frequently, until it softens.

4 Add the remaining fish stock and bring to the boil. Slowly whisk in the flour mixture until well combined and bring back to the boil, whisking constantly. Add the mussel cooking liquid. Season with salt, if needed, and pepper. Reduce the heat and simmer, partially covered, for 15 minutes.

5 Add the fish and mussels and continue simmering, stirring occasionally, for about 5 minutes or until the fish is cooked and begins to flake.

6 Stir in the prawns and cream. Taste and adjust the seasoning. Simmer for a few minutes to heat through. Ladle into warmed bowls, garnish with dill and lemon and serve.

This soup is swimming with seafood. Depending on availability, you could substitute skinless, boneless white fish for the scallops or prawns.

Shellfish *and* Tomato Soup

1 Discard any broken mussels and those with open shells that do not close when tapped. Rinse, pull off any 'beards', and if there are barnacles, scrape them off with a knife under cold running water. Put the mussels in a large heavy-based saucepan, cover tightly and cook over a high heat for 4–5 minutes or until the mussels open, shaking the pan occasionally.

2 Remove the mussels from the shells, adding additional juices to the cooking liquid. Strain the liquid through a muslin-lined sieve. Top it up with water to make 450 ml/16 fl oz.

3 Melt the butter in a large saucepan over a medium-low heat. Add the shallots and cook for 3–4 minutes, stirring frequently, until soft. Stir in the flour and continue cooking for 2 minutes. Add the wine.

4 Slowly add the fish stock and stir well, scraping the bottom of the pan to mix in the flour. Pour in the remaining mussel cooking liquid and water and bring just to the boil, stirring frequently. Reduce the heat, cover and simmer for 10 minutes.

5 Add the scallops, prawns and mussels, and continue cooking for 1 minute.

6 Stir in the cream, tomatoes, chives and most of the parsley. Season to taste with salt. Sprinkle with the remaining parsley and serve.

SERVES 4

1 kg/2 lb 4 oz mussels
25 g/1 oz butter
2 shallots, chopped finely
4 tbsp plain flour
4 tbsp dry white wine
600 ml/1 pint fish stock
200 g/7 oz queen scallops
200 g/7 oz cooked peeled prawns
125 ml/4 fl oz double cream
4 tomatoes, peeled, deseeded and chopped
2 tbsp snipped fresh chives
2 tbsp chopped fresh parsley
salt and pepper

NUTRITION

Calories *316*; Sugars *3 g*; Protein *26 g*; Carbohydrate *21 g*; Fat *14 g*; Saturates *8 g*

 moderate

15 mins

35 mins

For this tasty and unusual soup, boneless leg is a good cut of beef to use, as it is generally lean and any fat is easily trimmed off.

Mexican-style Beef *and* Rice Soup

SERVES 4

3 tbsp olive oil
500 g/1 lb 2 oz boneless stewing beef, cut into 2.5-cm/1-inch pieces
150 ml/5 fl oz red wine
1 onion, chopped finely
1 green pepper, cored, deseeded and chopped finely
1 small fresh red chilli, deseeded and chopped finely
2 garlic cloves, chopped finely
1 carrot, chopped finely
¼ tsp ground coriander
¼ tsp ground cumin
¼ tsp dried oregano
⅛ tsp ground cinnamon
1 bay leaf
grated rind of ½ orange
400 g/14 oz canned chopped tomatoes
1.2 litres/2 pints beef stock
50 g/1¾ oz long-grain white rice
25 g/1 oz raisins
15 g/½ oz plain chocolate, melted
chopped fresh coriander, to garnish

NUTRITION

Calories *501*; Sugars *14 g*; Protein *45 g*; Carbohydrate *36 g*; Fat *18 g*; Saturates *5 g*

easy

15 mins

2 hrs

1 Heat half the oil in a large frying pan over a medium-high heat. Add the meat in one layer and cook until well browned, turning to colour all sides. Remove the pan from the heat and pour in the wine.

2 Heat the remaining oil in a large saucepan over a medium heat. Add the onion, cover and cook for about 3 minutes, stirring occasionally, until just softened. Add the green pepper, chilli, garlic and carrot, and continue cooking, covered, for 3 minutes.

3 Add the ground coriander, cumin, oregano, cinnamon, bay leaf and orange rind. Stir in the tomatoes and stock, along with the beef and wine. Bring almost to the boil and when the mixture begins to bubble, reduce the heat to low. Cover and simmer gently, stirring occasionally, for about 1 hour or until the meat is tender.

4 Stir in the rice, raisins and chocolate, and continue cooking, stirring occasionally, for about 30 minutes or until the rice and beef are tender.

5 Ladle into warmed bowls and garnish with fresh coriander.

Spicy or smoky sausages add substance to this soup, which makes a hearty and warming supper, served with crusty bread and green salad.

Cabbage Soup *with* Sausage

1 Put the sausages in water to cover generously and bring to the boil. Reduce the heat and simmer until firm. Drain the sausages and, when cool enough to handle, remove the skin, if you wish, and slice thinly.

2 Heat the oil in a large saucepan over a medium heat, add the onion, leek and carrots and cook for 3–4 minutes, stirring frequently, until the onion starts to soften.

3 Add the tomatoes, cabbage, garlic, thyme, stock and sausages. Bring to the boil, reduce the heat to low and cook gently, partially covered, for about 40 minutes or until the vegetables are tender.

4 Taste the soup and adjust the seasoning, if necessary. Ladle into warmed bowls and serve with Parmesan cheese.

SERVES 6

350 g/12 oz lean sausages, preferably highly seasoned
2 tsp oil
1 onion, chopped finely
1 leek, halved lengthways and sliced thinly
2 carrots, halved and sliced thinly
400 g/14 oz canned chopped tomatoes
350 g/12 oz young green cabbage, cored and shredded coarsely
1-2 garlic cloves, chopped finely
pinch of dried thyme
1.5 litres/2¾ pints chicken or meat stock
salt and pepper
freshly grated Parmesan cheese, to serve

NUTRITION

Calories *160*; Sugars *7 g*; Protein *10 g*; Carbohydrate *12 g*; Fat *8 g*; Saturates *1 g*

★★★   moderate
🕐   10 mins
🕐   1 hr 15 mins

 COOK'S TIP

If you don't have fresh stock available, use water instead, with 1 stock cube only dissolved in it. Add a little more onion and garlic, plus a bouquet garni (remove it before serving).

This soup is perfect for the sweet meat of rabbit, which is traditionally paired with tomatoes and mushrooms.

Hunter's Soup

SERVES 4

1–2 tbsp olive oil
900 g/2 lb rabbit, jointed
1 onion, chopped finely
2–3 garlic cloves, chopped finely or crushed
100 g/3½ oz lean smoked back bacon, chopped finely
125 ml/4 fl oz white wine
1.2 litres/2 pints chicken stock
450 ml/16 fl oz tomato juice
2 tbsp tomato purée
2 carrots, halved lengthways and sliced
1 bay leaf
¼ tsp dried thyme
¼ tsp dried oregano
15 g/½ oz butter
300 g/10½ oz mushrooms, sliced or quartered if small
salt and pepper
chopped fresh parsley, to garnish

NUTRITION
Calories 377; Sugars 13 g; Protein 36 g; Carbohydrate 16 g; Fat 17 g; Saturates 6 g

 moderate

20 mins

1 hr 30 mins

1 Heat the oil in a large pan over a medium heat. Add the rabbit, in batches if necessary, and cook until lightly browned on all sides, adding a little more oil if needed. Remove from the pan.

2 Reduce the heat slightly and add the onion, garlic and bacon to the pan. Cook, stirring frequently, for a further 2 minutes or until the onion has softened.

3 Add the wine and simmer for 1 minute. Add the stock and return the rabbit to the pan with any juices. Bring to the boil and skim off any foam that rises to the surface.

4 Reduce the heat and stir in the tomato juice, tomato purée, carrots, bay leaf, thyme and oregano. Season with salt and pepper. Cover and simmer gently for 1 hour or until very tender.

5 Remove the rabbit pieces with a draining spoon and, when cool enough to handle, remove the meat from the bones. Discard any fat or gristle, along with the bones. Cut the meat into bite-sized pieces and return to the soup.

6 Melt the butter in a frying pan over a medium-high heat. Add the mushrooms and season with salt and pepper. Fry gently until lightly golden, then add to the soup. Simmer for 10-15 minutes to blend. Season to taste and serve sprinkled with parsley.

This delicately curried chicken soup requires a flavourful stock. Its velvety texture makes it an elegant starter.

Senegalese Soup

1 Heat the stock in a large saucepan. Add the onion, carrot, celery, apple, garlic and curry powder with a large pinch of salt, if the stock is unsalted. Bring to the boil, reduce the heat and simmer, covered, for 20 minutes.

2 Trim any fat from the chicken. Add the chicken to the stock and continue simmering for 10 minutes or until the chicken is tender. Remove the chicken with a slotted spoon.

3 Strain the stock and discard the stock vegetables. Spoon off any fat. When cool enough to handle, cut the chicken into thin slivers.

4 Put the strained stock in a large heavy-based saucepan and put over a medium heat. When starting to bubble around the edge, adjust the heat so it continues to bubble gently at the edge but remains still in the centre.

5 Put the egg yolks in a bowl. Add the cornflour and cream and whisk until smooth. Whisk one-quarter of the hot stock into the cream mixture, then pour it all back into the saucepan, whisking constantly. With a wooden spoon, stir constantly for 10 minutes or until the soup thickens slightly. Do not allow it to boil or the soup may curdle. If you see the soup beginning to boil, take the pan off the heat and stir more quickly until it cools down.

6 Stir in the chicken and reduce the heat to low. Season the soup with salt, pepper and nutmeg. Ladle into warmed soup bowls, garnish with toasted coconut strips or pecans and serve.

SERVES 4

1.2 litres/2 pints chicken stock
1 small onion, sliced thinly
1 small carrot, chopped finely
1 celery stick, chopped finely
½ small eating apple, peeled, cored and chopped
1–2 garlic cloves, halved
1 tsp mild curry powder
200 g/7 oz skinless, boneless chicken breast
2 egg yolks
4 tbsp cornflour
225 ml/8 fl oz whipping cream
freshly grated nutmeg
salt and white pepper
toasted coconut strips or pecans, to garnish

NUTRITION
Calories *428*; Sugars *6 g*; Protein *16 g*; Carbohydrate *34 g*; Fat *26 g*; Saturates *15 g*

 moderate

15 mins

40 mins

This soup contains okra, an essential ingredient in a gumbo. It helps thicken the soup, which starts with the traditional Cajun base of cooked flour and oil.

Chicken Gumbo Soup

SERVES 6

2 tbsp olive oil
4 tbsp plain flour
1 onion, chopped finely
1 small green pepper, cored, deseeded
    and chopped finely
1 celery stick, chopped finely
1.2 litres/2 pints chicken stock
400 g/14 oz canned chopped tomatoes
    in juice
3 garlic cloves, chopped finely or crushed
125 g/4½ oz okra, stems removed,
    cut into 5 mm/¼ inch thick slices
50 g/1¾ oz white rice
200 g/7 oz cooked chicken, cubed
115 g/4 oz cooked garlic sausage,
    sliced or cubed

1 Heat the oil in a large heavy-based saucepan over a medium-low heat and stir in the flour to make the roux. Cook for about 15 minutes, stirring occasionally, until the mixture is a rich golden brown (see Cook's Tip).

2 Add the onion, green pepper and celery and continue cooking for about 10 minutes or until the onion softens.

3 Slowly pour in the stock and bring to the boil, stirring well and scraping the bottom of the pan to mix in the flour. Remove the pan from the heat.

4 Add the tomatoes and garlic. Stir in the okra and rice and season. Reduce the heat, cover and simmer for 20 minutes or until the okra is tender.

5 Add the chicken and sausage and continue simmering for about 10 minutes. Taste and adjust the seasoning, if necessary, and ladle into warmed bowls.

NUTRITION

Calories 242; Sugars 5 g; Protein 17 g;
Carbohydrate 23 g; Fat 10 g; Saturates 2 g

easy

15 mins

1 hr

 COOK'S TIP

Keep a watchful eye on the roux as it begins to darken. The soup gains a lot of flavour from this traditional Cajun base, but if it burns the soup will be bitter. If you prefer, soften the onion, green pepper and celery in the oil, then add the flour.

This soup uses the colourful dried bean mixes available that include a variety of different beans. Brightly coloured vegetables are added for a lively combination.

Confetti Bean Soup

1 Pick over the beans, cover generously with cold water and leave to soak for 6 hours or overnight. Drain the beans, put in a saucepan and add enough cold water to cover by 5 cm/2 inches. Bring to the boil and boil for 10 minutes, skimming off the foam as it accumulates. Drain and rinse well.

2 Heat the oil in a large saucepan over a medium heat. Add the onions and pepper, cover and cook for 3–4 minutes, stirring occasionally, until the onion is just softened. Add the garlic, carrots, parsnip, celery and gammon or ham and continue cooking for 2–3 minutes or until the onion begins to colour.

3 Add the water, drained beans, tomato purée, thyme and bay leaf. Bring just to the boil, cover and simmer, occasionally stirring, for 1¼ hours or until the beans and vegetables are tender.

4 Put the potato in a small saucepan and ladle over just enough of the bean cooking liquid to cover. Bring to the boil, cover the pan, reduce the heat and boil gently for about 12 minutes or until the potato is very tender.

5 Put the potato and its cooking liquid into a blender or food processor, then add 3 ladlefuls of the beans with a small amount of their liquid and purée until completely smooth.

6 Scrape the purée into the saucepan, add the marjoram and parsley and stir to blend. Season the soup to taste, adding salt and pepper generously. Reheat gently over a medium-low heat until hot and ladle the soup into warmed bowls.

SERVES 8

500 g/1 lb 2 oz mixed dried beans
1 tbsp olive oil
2 onions, chopped finely
1 yellow or orange pepper, cored, deseeded and chopped finely
3 garlic cloves, chopped finely or crushed
2 carrots, cubed
1 parsnip, cubed
2 celery sticks, halved lengthways and cut into 5 mm/¼ inch pieces
100 g/3½ oz lean smoked gammon or ham, cubed
2 litres/3½ pints water
2 tbsp tomato purée
⅛ tsp dried thyme
1 bay leaf
1 potato, diced finely
1 tbsp chopped fresh marjoram
2 tbsp chopped fresh parsley
salt and pepper

NUTRITION

Calories 241; Sugars 6 g; Protein 16 g; Carbohydrate 41 g; Fat 4 g; Saturates 0 g

moderate

15 mins

1 hr 45 mins

Pumpkin, a greatly underrated vegetable, balances the spicy heat in this soup and gives it a splash of colour, too.

Bean *and* Pumpkin Soup

SERVES 4

250 g/9 oz dried kidney beans
1 tbsp olive oil
2 onions, chopped finely
4 garlic cloves, chopped finely
1 celery stick, sliced thinly
1 carrot, halved and sliced thinly
2 tsp tomato purée
pinch of dried thyme
pinch of dried oregano
pinch of ground cumin
1.2 litres/2 pints water
1 bay leaf
400 g/14 oz canned chopped tomatoes
250 g/9 oz peeled pumpkin flesh, diced
¼ tsp chilli purée
salt and pepper
fresh coriander leaves, to garnish

1 Pick over the beans, cover generously with cold water and set aside to soak for 6 hours or overnight. Drain the beans, put in a pan and add enough cold water to cover by 5 cm/2 inches. Bring to the boil and boil for 10 minutes. Drain and rinse.

2 Heat the olive oil in a large pan over a medium heat. Add the onions and cook, stirring occasionally, for 3–4 minutes or until they are just softened. Add the garlic, celery and carrot and continue cooking for 2 minutes.

3 Add the kidney beans, tomato purée, thyme, oregano, cumin, water and bay leaf. When the mixture is just beginning to simmer, reduce the heat to low. Cover and simmer gently, stirring occasionally, for 1 hour.

4 Stir in the tomatoes, pumpkin and chilli purée. Continue simmering, stirring occasionally, for about 1 hour more or until the beans and pumpkin are tender.

5 Season the soup to taste with salt and pepper and stir in a little more chilli purée, if liked. Ladle the soup into warmed bowls, garnish with coriander leaves and serve immediately.

NUTRITION
Calories *170*; Sugars *8 g*; Protein *11 g*;
Carbohydrate *27 g*; Fat *3 g*; Saturates *0 g*

easy

6 hrs 15 mins

2 hrs 30 mins

This soup is satisfying and very healthy. Brown rice gives a pleasing chewy texture, but white rice could be used instead.

Rice *and* Bean Soup

1 Put the beans in a bowl, cover generously with cold water and set aside to soak for at least 6 hours or overnight. Drain the beans, put in a pan and add enough cold water to cover by 5 cm/2 inches. Bring to the boil and boil for 10 minutes. Drain and rinse well.

2 Heat the oil in a large heavy-based pan over a medium heat. Add the onion, cover and cook, stirring frequently, for 3–4 minutes or until just softened. Add the garlic, carrots, celery and pepper, stir well and cook for a further 2 minutes.

3 Transfer to a larger pan if necessary. Add the beans, ham, thyme, bay leaf, stock and water. Bring to the boil, reduce the heat, cover and simmer gently, stirring occasionally, for 1 hour or until the beans are just tender.

4 Stir in the rice and season the soup with salt, if needed, and pepper. Continue cooking for 30 minutes or until the rice and beans are tender.

5 Remove and discard the bay leaf. Taste the soup and adjust the seasoning if necessary. Ladle into warmed bowls and serve garnished with parsley or chives.

SERVES 4

250 g/9 oz dried black-eye beans
1 tbsp olive oil
1 large onion, chopped finely
2 garlic cloves, chopped finely or crushed
2 carrots, chopped finely
2 celery sticks, chopped finely
1 small red pepper, deseeded and chopped finely
85 g/3 oz lean smoked ham, diced finely
1/2 tsp fresh thyme leaves
1 bay leaf
1.2 litres/2 pints chicken or vegetable stock
600 ml/1 pint water
100 g/3 1/2 oz brown rice
salt and pepper
chopped fresh parsley or chives, to garnish

NUTRITION

Calories *285*; Sugars *7 g*; Protein *18 g*; Carbohydrate *43 g*; Fat *5 g*; Saturates *1 g*

⭐⭐ easy

🕐 6 hrs 15 mins

 2 hrs

Traditional Soups

The soups found in this chapter are guaranteed to provide good old-fashioned nourishment and are perfect served as a main course accompanied by a hearty chunk of fresh bread or perhaps a salad or a wedge of strong tasting cheese. Wholesome treats include traditional recipes for Scotch Broth, Lentil and Ham Soup and delicious Mushroom and Barley Soup. To make the most of these soups, remember that they are only as good as their ingredients, so be sure to pick good quality produce.

It is hard to imagine that celeriac, a coarse, knobbly vegetable, can taste so sweet. It makes a wonderfully flavourful soup.

Celeriac, Leek *and* Potato Soup

SERVES 4

15 g/½ oz butter
1 onion, chopped
2 large leeks, halved lengthways and sliced
1 large celeriac (about 750 g/1 lb 10 oz), peeled and cubed
1 potato, cubed
1 carrot, quartered and sliced thinly
1.2 litres/2 pints water
⅛ tsp dried marjoram
1 bay leaf
freshly grated nutmeg
salt and pepper
celery leaves, to garnish

1 Melt the butter in a large saucepan over a medium-low heat. Add the onion and leeks and cook for about 4 minutes, stirring frequently, until just softened; do not allow to colour.

2 Add the celeriac, potato, carrot, water, marjoram and bay leaf, with a large pinch of salt. Bring to the boil, reduce the heat, cover and simmer for about 25 minutes or until the vegetables are tender. Remove the bay leaf.

3 Allow the soup to cool slightly. Transfer to a blender or food processor and purée until smooth. (If using a food processor, strain off the cooking liquid and reserve. Purée the soup solids with enough cooking liquid to moisten them, then combine with remaining liquid.)

4 Return the puréed soup to the saucepan and stir to blend. Season with salt, pepper and nutmeg. Simmer over a medium-low heat until reheated.

5 Ladle the soup into warmed bowls, garnish with celery leaves and serve.

NUTRITION
Calories 20; Sugars 1.3 g; Protein 1 g; Carbohydrate 3 g; Fat 0.7 g; Saturates 0.4 g

moderate

10 mins

35 mins

This unusual baked soup is perfect for lunch on a crisp, cold winter's day – pop it in the oven and enjoy a brisk walk while it is cooking.

Baked Leek *and* Cabbage Soup

1 Melt the butter in a large saucepan over a medium heat. Add the leeks and onion and cook for 4–5 minutes, stirring frequently, until just softened.

2 Add the garlic and cabbage, stir to combine and continue cooking for about 5 minutes until the cabbage has just wilted.

3 Stir in the stock and simmer the soup for 10 minutes. Taste and season with salt and pepper.

4 Arrange the bread in the base of a large deep 3 litre/5¼ pint ovenproof dish. Sprinkle about half the cheese over the bread.

5 Ladle over the soup and top with the remaining cheese. Bake in a preheated oven at 180°C/350°F/Gas Mark 4 for 1 hour. Ladle the soup into warmed bowls, garnish with parsley and serve.

SERVES 4

25 g/1 oz butter
2 large leeks, halved lengthways and sliced thinly
1 large onion, halved and sliced thinly
3 garlic cloves, chopped finely
250 g/9 oz finely shredded green cabbage
1 litre/1¾ pints vegetable stock
4 slices firm bread, cut in half, or 8 slices baguette
250 g/9 oz Gruyère cheese, grated
salt and pepper
parsley leaves, to garnish

NUTRITION
Calories *420*; Sugars *8 g*; Protein *24 g*; Carbohydrate *27 g*; Fat *25 g*; Saturates *15 g*

★★★ moderate
🕐 15 mins
🕐 1 hr 25 mins

 COOK'S TIP

A large soufflé dish or earthenware casserole at least 10 cm/4 inches deep, or an enamelled cast-iron casserole, is good for baking the soup. If necessary, put a baking sheet with a rim underneath to catch any overflow.

A chunky soup, ideal for a snack or a quick lunch. Save some of the soup and purée it to make one portion of creamed soup for the next day.

Leek, Potato *and* Carrot Soup

SERVES 2

1 leek, about 175 g/6 oz
1 tbsp sunflower oil
1 garlic clove, crushed
700 ml/1¼ pints vegetable stock
1 bay leaf
¼ tsp ground cumin
175 g/6 oz potatoes, diced
125 g/4½ oz coarsely grated carrot
salt and pepper
chopped parsley, to garnish

puréed soup
5–6 tbsp milk
1–2 tbsp double cream, crème fraîche
    or soured cream

1 Trim off and discard some of the coarse green part of the leek, then slice the leek thinly and rinse thoroughly in cold water. Drain well.

2 Heat the sunflower oil in a heavy-based saucepan. Add the leek and garlic and cook over a low heat for about 2–3 minutes or until soft, but barely coloured. Add the vegetable stock, bay leaf and cumin and season to taste with salt and pepper. Bring the mixture to the boil, stirring constantly.

3 Add the diced potato to the saucepan, cover and simmer over a low heat for 10–15 minutes. Keep a careful eye on the soup during the cooking time to make sure the potato cooks until it is just tender, but not broken up.

4 Add the grated carrot to the pan and simmer the soup for a further 2–3 minutes. Adjust the seasoning if necessary, discard the bay leaf and serve the soup in warmed bowls, sprinkled liberally with chopped parsley.

5 To make a puréed soup, first process the leftovers (about half the original soup) in a blender or food processor, or press through a sieve with the back of a wooden spoon until smooth, then return to a clean saucepan with the milk. Bring to the boil and simmer for 2–3 minutes.

6 Adjust the seasoning and stir in the cream or crème fraîche before serving the soup in warmed bowls, sprinkled with chopped parsley.

NUTRITION
Calories *156*; Sugars *7 g*; Protein *4 g*;
Carbohydrate *22 g*; Fat *6 g*; Saturates *0.7 g*

          very easy

                      10 mins

                      25 mins

Cauliflower can taste rather bland, but using dry cider in this creamy soup gives it an unusual kick.

Cauliflower *and* Cider Soup

1 Melt the butter in a saucepan over a medium heat. Add the onion and garlic and cook for about 5 minutes, stirring occasionally, until just softened.

2 Add the carrot and cauliflower to the pan and pour over the cider. Season with salt, pepper and a generous grating of nutmeg. Bring to the boil, then reduce the heat to low. Cover and cook very gently for about 50 minutes or until the vegetables are very soft.

3 Allow the soup to cool slightly, then transfer to a blender or food processor and purée until smooth, working in batches if necessary. (If using a food processor, strain off the cooking liquid and reserve. Purée the soup solids with enough cooking liquid to moisten them, then combine with the remaining liquid.)

4 Return the soup to the saucepan and stir in the milk and cream. Taste and adjust the seasoning, if necessary. Simmer the soup over a low heat, stirring occasionally, until heated through.

5 Ladle the soup into warmed bowls, garnish with chives and serve.

SERVES 4

25 g/1 oz butter
1 onion, chopped finely
1 garlic clove, crushed
1 carrot, sliced thinly
500 g/1 lb 2 oz cauliflower florets (from 1 medium head)
600 ml/1 pint dry cider
freshly grated nutmeg
125 ml/4 fl oz milk
125 ml/4 fl oz double cream
salt and pepper
snipped fresh chives, to garnish

NUTRITION
Calories *312*; Sugars *13 g*; Protein *7 g*; Carbohydrate *15 g*; Fat *21 g*; Saturates *13 g*

⭐⭐⭐   moderate

🖐   15 mins

🕐   1 hr

👨‍🍳 COOK'S TIP

If you don't have dry cider, substitute 200 ml/7 fl oz each white wine, apple juice and water.

Fresh asparagus is now available for most of the year, so this soup can be made at any time. It can also be made using canned asparagus.

Asparagus Soup

SERVES 4

1 bunch asparagus, about 350 g/12 oz, or 2 packs mini asparagus, about 150 g/5½ oz each
700 ml/1¼ pints vegetable stock
60 g/2 oz butter or margarine
1 onion, chopped
3 tbsp plain flour
¼ tsp ground coriander
1 tbsp lemon juice
450 ml/16 fl oz milk
4–6 tbsp double or single cream
salt and pepper

NUTRITION
Calories 196; Sugars 7 g; Protein 7 g;
Carbohydrate 15 g; Fat 12 g; Saturates 4 g

⭐ very easy

🕐 5–10 mins

🕐 55 mins

1 Wash and trim the asparagus, discarding the lower, woody part of the stem. Cut the remainder into short lengths, keeping aside a few tips to use as a garnish. Mini asparagus does not need to be trimmed.

2 Cook the tips in the minimum of boiling salted water for 5–10 minutes. Drain and set aside.

3 Put the asparagus stems in a saucepan with the stock, bring to the boil, cover and simmer for about 20 minutes or until soft. Drain and reserve the stock.

4 Melt the butter or margarine in a saucepan. Add the onion and cook over a low heat until soft, but only barely coloured. Stir in the flour and cook for 1 minute, then gradually whisk in the reserved stock and bring to the boil.

5 Simmer for 2–3 minutes or until thickened, then stir in the cooked asparagus, seasoning, coriander and lemon juice. Simmer for 10 minutes, then cool a little and either press through a sieve with the back of a spoon or process in a blender or food processor until smooth.

6 Pour into a clean pan, add the milk and reserved asparagus tips and bring to the boil. Simmer for 2 minutes. Stir in the cream, reheat gently and serve.

 COOK'S TIP

If using canned asparagus, drain off the liquid and use as part of the measured stock. Remove a few small asparagus tips for garnish and chop the remainder. Continue as above.

This old-fashioned soup is nourishing and warming, with distinctive flavours and a nice chewy texture.

Mushroom *and* Barley Soup

1 Rinse and drain the barley. Bring 450 ml/16 fl oz of the stock to the boil in a small pan. Add the bay leaf and a pinch of salt. Stir in the barley, reduce the heat, cover and simmer for 40 minutes.

2 Melt the butter in a large frying pan over a medium heat. Add the mushrooms and season to taste with salt and pepper. Cook, stirring occasionally, for about 8 minutes or until they are golden brown. Stir more often after the mushrooms start to colour. Remove the mushrooms from the heat.

3 Heat the oil in a large pan over a medium heat and add the onion and carrots. Cook, stirring occasionally, for about 3 minutes or until the onion is softened and translucent.

4 Add the remaining stock and bring to the boil. Stir in the barley with its cooking liquid and add the mushrooms. Reduce the heat, cover and simmer gently, stirring occasionally, for about 20 minutes or until the carrots are tender.

5 Stir in the chopped tarragon and parsley. Ladle into warmed bowls, garnish with fresh parsley or tarragon and serve.

COOK'S TIP

The barley will continue to absorb liquid if the soup is stored, so if you are making ahead, you may need to add a little more stock or water when reheating the soup.

SERVES 4

60 g/2 oz pearl barley
1.5 litres/2³/₄ pints chicken or vegetable stock
1 bay leaf
15 g/¹/₂ oz butter
350 g/12 oz mushrooms, sliced thinly
1 tsp olive oil
1 onion, chopped finely
2 carrots, sliced thinly
1 tbsp chopped fresh tarragon
1 tbsp chopped fresh parsley
salt and pepper
1 tbsp fresh parsley or tarragon leaves, to garnish

NUTRITION
Calories *204*; Sugars *7 g*; Protein *5 g*;
Carbohydrate *31 g*; Fat *8 g*; Saturates *3 g*

 moderate
 5 mins
1 hr 15 mins

Crisp, fresh celery and creamy Stilton cheese are a delicious combination, which works very well in soup.

Celery *and* Stilton Soup

SERVES 4

25 g/1 oz butter
1 onion, chopped finely
4 large celery sticks, peeled and chopped finely
1 large carrot, chopped finely
1 litre/1¾ pints vegetable stock
3–4 fresh thyme sprigs
1 bay leaf
125 ml/4 fl oz double cream
150 g/5½ oz Stilton cheese, crumbled
freshly grated nutmeg
salt and pepper
celery leaves, to garnish

NUTRITION
Calories *381*; Sugars *6 g*; Protein *10 g*;
Carbohydrate *7 g*; Fat *35 g*; Saturates *21 g*

moderate

15 mins

40 mins

1 Melt the butter in a large saucepan over a medium-low heat. Add the onion and cook for 3–4 minutes, stirring frequently, until just softened. Add the celery and carrot to the pan and continue cooking for 3 minutes. Season lightly with salt and pepper.

2 Add the stock, thyme and bay leaf and bring to the boil. Reduce the heat, cover and simmer gently for about 25 minutes, stirring occasionally, until the vegetables are very tender.

3 Allow the soup to cool slightly and remove the thyme and bay leaf. Transfer the soup to a blender or food processor and purée until smooth, working in batches if necessary. (If using a food processor, strain off the cooking liquid and reserve. Purée the soup solids with enough cooking liquid to moisten them, then combine with the remaining liquid.)

4 Return the puréed soup to the saucepan and stir in the cream. Simmer over a low heat for 5 minutes.

5 Add the Stilton slowly, stirring constantly, until smooth (do not allow the soup to boil). Taste and adjust the seasoning, adding salt, if needed, plenty of pepper and nutmeg to taste.

6 Ladle into warmed bowls, garnish with celery leaves and serve.

The cooking liquid in which the fish is poached becomes a delicious fish stock. If you just want stock, poach fish heads and trimmings instead of a whole fish.

Trout *and* Celeriac Soup

1 To make the fish stock base, melt the butter in a fish kettle, a large saucepan or cast-iron casserole over a medium-high heat. Add the onion, carrot and leek and cook for about 3 minutes or until the onion starts to soften.

2 Add the wine, water and bay leaf. Bring to the boil, reduce the heat a little, cover and boil gently for 15 minutes.

3 Put the fish into the liquid (if necessary, cut the fish in pieces to fit in). Bring back to the boil and skim off any foam that rises to the top. Reduce the heat to low and simmer gently for 20 minutes.

4 Remove the fish and set aside. Strain the stock through a muslin-lined sieve into a clean saucepan. Remove any fat from the stock. (There should be about 1.5 litres/2¾ pints stock.)

5 Bring the stock to the boil. Add the diced celeriac and boil gently, uncovered, for 15–20 minutes or until it is tender and the liquid has reduced by about one-third.

6 When the fish is cool enough to handle, peel off the skin and remove the flesh from the bones. Discard the skin, bones, head and tail.

7 Add the cream to the soup and when it comes back to the boil, stir in the dissolved cornflour. Boil gently for 2–3 minutes or until slightly thickened, stirring frequently. Return the fish to the soup. Cook for 3–4 minutes to reheat. Taste and adjust the seasoning, if necessary. Ladle into warmed bowls and garnish with chervil or parsley.

SERVES 4

700 g/1 lb 9 oz whole trout
200 g/7 oz celeriac, peeled and diced
150 ml/5 fl oz double cream
3 tbsp cornflour, dissolved in 3 tbsp water
chopped fresh chervil or parsley, to garnish

fish stock base
15 g/½ oz butter
l onion, sliced thinly
l carrot, sliced thinly
l leek, sliced thinly
225 ml/8 fl oz dry white wine
1.2 litres/2 pints water
1 bay leaf

NUTRITION
Calories *369*; Sugars *4 g*; Protein *24 g*;
Carbohydrate *17 g*; Fat *21 g*; Saturates *10 g*

✪✪✪ moderate

 25 mins

 1 hr 15 mins

Salmon is a favourite with almost everyone. This delicately flavoured and pretty soup is perfect for entertaining.

Salmon *and* Leek Soup

SERVES 4

1 tbsp olive oil
1 large onion, chopped finely
3 large leeks, including green parts,
    sliced thinly
1 potato, diced finely
450 ml/16 fl oz fish stock
700 ml/1¼ pints water
1 bay leaf
300 g/10½ oz skinless salmon fillet,
    cut into 1-cm/½-inch cubes
5 tbsp double cream
salt and pepper
fresh lemon juice, optional
fresh chervil or parsley sprigs, to garnish

1 Heat the oil in a heavy-based saucepan over a medium heat. Add the onion and leeks and cook for about 3 minutes or until they begin to soften.

2 Add the potato, stock, water and bay leaf with a large pinch of salt. Bring to the boil, reduce the heat, cover and cook gently for about 25 minutes or until the vegetables are tender. Remove the bay leaf.

3 Allow the soup to cool slightly, then transfer about half of it to a blender or food processor and purée until smooth. (If using a food processor, strain off the cooking liquid and reserve. Purée half the soup solids with enough cooking liquid to moisten them, then combine with the remaining liquid.)

4 Return the puréed soup to the saucepan and stir to blend. Reheat gently over a medium-low heat.

5 Season the salmon with salt and pepper and add to the soup. Continue cooking for about 5 minutes, stirring occasionally, until the fish is tender and starts to break up. Stir in the cream, taste and adjust the seasoning, adding a little lemon juice if wished. Ladle into warmed bowls, sprinkle with chervil or parsley and serve.

NUTRITION

Calories *338*; Sugars *7 g*; Protein *19 g*;
Carbohydrate *17 g*; Fat *22 g*; Saturates *8 g*

        moderate

10–15 mins

40 mins

This soup utilises every part of the prawns. If you wish, you could even leave the prawn flesh out of the soup because most of the flavour comes from the shells.

Prawn Bisque

1 Peel the prawns and keep the shells for the soup. Reserve the prawn flesh, covered, in the refrigerator.

2 Heat the oil in a large saucepan. Add the prawn shells and cook over a high heat, stirring frequently, until they start to brown. Reduce the heat and add one-quarter of the onions, the carrot, celery and garlic. Cover and cook for 4–5 minutes, stirring frequently, until the onions soften. Add the water and bay leaf with a small pinch of salt. Bring to the boil, reduce the heat, cover and simmer gently for 25 minutes. Strain the prawn stock.

3 Heat the butter in a large saucepan over a medium heat and add the remaining onions. Cover and cook for 5–6 minutes, stirring frequently, until they soften and just begin to colour. Add the prawn stock, rice and tomato purée. Bring to the boil. Reduce the heat, cover and simmer for 30 minutes or until the rice is very soft.

4 Allow the soup to cool slightly, then transfer to a blender or food processor and purée until smooth. (If using a food processor, strain off the cooking liquid and reserve. Purée the soup solids with enough cooking liquid to moisten them, then combine with the remaining liquid.)

5 Return the soup to the saucepan and place over a medium-low heat. Add the reserved prawns and a few drops of lemon juice, or to taste. Simmer for about 8 minutes, stirring occasionally, until the soup is reheated. Taste and adjust the seasoning if necessary. Ladle into warmed bowls, sprinkle with dill or parsley and serve.

SERVES 4

500 g/1 lb 2 oz cooked prawns in the shell
2 tsp oil
2 large onions, halved and sliced
1 carrot, grated
1 celery stick, sliced
1–2 garlic cloves, chopped finely or crushed
1.5 litres/2¾ pints water
1 bay leaf
10 g/⅓ oz butter
85 g/3 oz white rice
1 tbsp tomato purée
fresh lemon juice
salt and pepper
snipped fresh dill or chopped parsley,
    to garnish

NUTRITION
Calories 227; Sugars 7 g; Protein 25 g;
Carbohydrate 4 g; Fat 22 g; Saturates 1 g

✪✪✪   moderate
          15 mins
🕐   1 hr 20 mins

This light, lean soup is studded with small diced vegetables and fragrant herbs. The stock may be used as a basis for other soups.

Beef Broth

SERVES 4

200 g/7 oz celeriac, diced finely
2 large carrots, diced finely
2 tsp chopped fresh marjoram
2 tsp chopped fresh parsley
2 plum tomatoes, peeled, deseeded
    and diced
salt and pepper

beef stock

550 g/1 lb 4 oz boneless beef shin or
    stewing steak, cut into large cubes
750 g/1 lb 10 oz veal, beef or pork bones
2 onions, quartered
2.5 litres/4½ pints water
4 garlic cloves, sliced
2 carrots, sliced
1 large leek, sliced
1 celery stick, cut into 5-cm/2-inch pieces
1 bay leaf
4–5 fresh thyme sprigs or ¼ tsp dried thyme
salt

NUTRITION

Calories *21*; Sugars *3 g*; Protein *1 g*;
Carbohydrate *4 g*; Fat *1 g*; Saturates *0 g*

 moderate

15 mins

5 hrs 15 mins

1 To make the stock, trim the fat from the beef and put the beef and the fat into a large roasting tin with the bones and onions. Roast in a preheated oven at 190°C/375°F/Gas Mark 5 for 30–40 minutes or until browned, turning once or twice. Transfer the ingredients to a large flameproof casserole and discard the beef fat.

2 Add the water (it should cover by at least 5 cm/2 inches) and bring to the boil. Skim off any foam, reduce the heat and add the garlic, carrots, leek, celery, bay leaf, thyme and a pinch of salt. Simmer very gently for 4 hours, skimming occasionally. If the ingredients emerge from the liquid, top up with water.

3 Strain the stock through a muslin-lined sieve into a large container and remove as much fat as possible. Save the meat for another purpose, if wished, and discard the bones and vegetables.

4 Simmer the stock very gently until it is reduced to 1.5 litres/2¾ pints. Taste and adjust the seasoning if necessary.

5 Bring a pan of salted water to the boil and add the celeriac and carrots. Reduce the heat, cover and simmer for about 15 minutes or until tender. Drain.

6 Add the herbs to the boiling beef stock. Divide the cooked vegetables and tomatoes between warmed bowls, ladle over the stock and serve.

This traditional winter soup is full of goodness, with lots of tasty golden vegetables along with tender barley and lamb.

Scotch Broth

1 Rinse the barley under cold running water. Put in a pan and add water to cover generously. Bring to the boil over a medium heat and boil for 3 minutes, skimming off the foam from the surface. Remove the pan from the heat, cover and set aside.

2 Put the lamb in another large pan with the measured water and bring to the boil. Skim off the foam that rises to the surface.

3 Stir in the garlic, stock, onion and bay leaf. Reduce the heat, partially cover and simmer for 15 minutes.

4 Drain the barley and add to the soup. Add the leek, carrots, parsnip and swede. Simmer, stirring occasionally, for about 1 hour or until the lamb and vegetables are tender.

5 Season to taste with salt and pepper, stir in the parsley and serve.

SERVES 4

55 g/2 oz pearl barley
300 g/10½ oz lean boneless lamb, such as shoulder or neck fillet, trimmed of fat and cut into 1-cm/½-inch cubes
700 ml/1¼ pints water
2 garlic cloves, chopped finely or crushed
1 litre/1¾ pints chicken or meat stock
1 onion, chopped finely
1 bay leaf
1 large leek, quartered lengthways and sliced
2 large carrots, diced finely
1 parsnip, diced finely
125 g/4½ oz swede, diced
2 tbsp chopped fresh parsley
salt and pepper

NUTRITION
Calories *186*; Sugars *6 g*; Protein *13 g*; Carbohydrate *23 g*; Fat *5 g*; Saturates *2 g*

★★★ moderate
🕐 10–15 mins
🕐 1 hr 30 mins

🍴 COOK'S TIP

This soup is lean when the lamb is trimmed. By making it beforehand, you can remove any hardened fat before reheating.

A thick vegetable soup which is a delicious meal in itself. Serve the soup with thin shavings of Parmesan and warm ciabatta bread.

Winter Soup

SERVES 4

2 tbsp olive oil
2 leeks, sliced thinly
2 courgettes, chopped
2 garlic cloves, crushed
800 g/28 oz canned chopped tomatoes
1 tbsp tomato purée
1 bay leaf
900 ml/1½ pints vegetable stock
400 g/14 oz canned chick peas, drained
225 g/8 oz spinach
25 g/1 oz Parmesan cheese, shaved thinly
salt and pepper
crusty bread, to serve

1 Heat the oil in a heavy-based saucepan. Add the sliced leeks and courgettes and cook over a medium heat, stirring constantly, for 5 minutes.

2 Add the garlic, chopped tomatoes, tomato purée, bay leaf, vegetable stock and chick peas. Bring to the boil, reduce the heat and simmer, stirring occasionally, for 5 minutes.

3 Shred the spinach finely and add it to the soup. Cook the soup for a further 2 minutes over a medium-high heat, until the spinach is just wilted. Season to taste with salt and pepper.

4 Remove the bay leaf. Pour the soup into a warmed tureen or individual bowls and sprinkle over the Parmesan. Serve with crusty bread.

NUTRITION
Calories 285; Sugars 11 g; Protein 16 g;
Carbohydrate 29 g; Fat 12 g; Saturates 3 g

 very easy

 10 mins

 20 mins

Warming and nutritious, this broth is perfect for a cold winter's day. The slow cooking allows you to use one of the cheaper cuts of meat.

Lamb *and* Barley Broth

1 Heat the vegetable oil in a large, heavy-based saucepan and add the pieces of lamb, turning them to seal and brown on both sides.

2 Lift the lamb out of the pan and set aside until required.

3 Add the onion, carrots and leeks to the saucepan and cook gently for about 3 minutes.

4 Return the lamb to the saucepan and add the vegetable stock, bay leaf, parsley and pearl barley to the saucepan.

5 Bring the mixture in the pan to the boil, then reduce the heat. Cover and simmer for 1½ –2 hours.

6 Discard the parsley sprigs. Lift the pieces of lamb from the broth and allow them to cool slightly.

7 Remove the bones and any fat and chop the meat. Return the lamb to the broth and reheat gently.

8 Ladle the lamb and parsley broth into warmed bowls and serve immediately.

SERVES 4

1 tbsp vegetable oil
500 g/1 lb 2 oz lean neck of lamb, cut into 2.5-cm/1-inch cubes
1 large onion, sliced
2 carrots, sliced
2 leeks, sliced
1 litre/1¾ pints vegetable stock
1 bay leaf
few fresh parsley sprigs
60 g/2 oz pearl barley

NUTRITION

Calories *304*; Sugars *4 g*; Protein *29 g*; Carbohydrate *16 g*; Fat *14 g*; Saturates *6 g*

easy
15 mins
2 hrs 15 mins

🍳 COOK'S TIP

This broth will taste even better if made the day before, as this allows the flavours to develop fully. It also means that any fat will solidify on the surface so you can then lift it off. Keep the broth in the refrigerator until required.

Smooth and delicious, this soup has the most glorious golden colour and a fabulous flavour.

Lentil *and* Parsnip Pottage

SERVES 4

3 slices lean streaky bacon, chopped
1 onion, chopped
2 carrots, chopped
2 parsnips, chopped
60 g/2 oz red lentils
1 litre/1¾ pints vegetable stock or water
salt and pepper
chopped fresh chives, to garnish

1 Heat a large saucepan, add the bacon and dry-fry for 5 minutes or until crisp and golden.

2 Add the chopped onion, carrots and parsnips and cook for about 5 minutes without browning.

3 Add the lentils to the saucepan and stir to mix with the vegetables.

4 Add the stock or water to the pan and bring to the boil. Cover and simmer for 30–40 minutes or until tender.

5 Transfer three-quarters of the soup to a blender or food processor and blend for about 15 seconds or until smooth. Alternatively, press the soup through a sieve.

6 Return to the reserved soup in the saucepan and reheat gently until almost boiling.

7 Season the soup with salt and pepper to taste.

8 Garnish the lentil and parsnip pottage with chopped fresh chives and serve at once.

NUTRITION
Calories *82*; Sugars *4 g*; Protein *6 g*;
Carbohydrate *13 g*; Fat *1 g*; Saturates *0.3 g*

 very easy

5 mins

55 mins

🍳 COOK'S TIP

For a meatier soup, use a knuckle of ham in place of the streaky bacon. Cook it for 1½–2 hours before adding the vegetables and lentils and use the ham's cooking liquid as the stock.

This is a good hearty soup, based on a stock made from a ham knuckle, with plenty of vegetables and red lentils to thicken it and add flavour.

Lentil *and* Ham Soup

1 Put the lentils and stock or water in a saucepan and leave to soak for 1–2 hours.

2 Add the onions, garlic, carrots, ham knuckle or bacon, tomatoes, bay leaves and seasoning.

3 Bring the mixture in the saucepan to the boil, cover and simmer for about 1 hour or until the lentils are tender, stirring occasionally to prevent the lentils from sticking to the bottom of the pan.

4 Add the potatoes and continue to simmer for about 20 minutes or until the potatoes and ham knuckle are tender.

5 Discard the bay leaves. Remove the knuckle and chop 125 g/4½ oz of the meat and reserve. If liked, press half the soup through a sieve or blend in a food processor or blender until smooth. Return to the pan with the rest of the soup.

6 Adjust the seasoning, add the vinegar and allspice and the reserved chopped ham. Simmer gently for a further 5–10 minutes. Serve sprinkled liberally with spring onions or chopped parsley.

SERVES 4

225 g/8 oz red lentils
1.5 litres/2¾ pints stock or water
2 onions, chopped
1 garlic clove, crushed
2 large carrots, chopped
1 lean ham knuckle or 175 g/6 oz lean bacon, chopped
4 large tomatoes, peeled and chopped
2 fresh or dried bay leaves
250 g/9 oz potatoes, chopped
1 tbsp white wine vinegar
¼ tsp ground allspice
salt and pepper
chopped spring onions or chopped fresh parsley, to garnish

NUTRITION

Calories *219*; Sugars *4 g*; Protein *17 g*; Carbohydrate *33 g*; Fat *3 g*; Saturates *1 g*

    easy

   2 hrs 15 mins

   1 hr 45 mins

This is a real winter warmer – pieces of tender beef and chunky mixed vegetables are cooked in a stock flavoured with sherry.

Chunky Potato *and* Beef Soup

SERVES 4

2 tbsp vegetable oil
225 g/8 oz lean braising or frying steak, cut into strips
225 g/8 oz new potatoes, halved
1 carrot, diced
2 celery sticks, sliced
2 leeks, sliced
850 ml/1½ pints beef stock
8 baby corn cobs, sliced
1 bouquet garni
2 tbsp dry sherry
salt and pepper
chopped fresh parsley, to garnish
crusty bread, to serve

1 Heat the vegetable oil in a large pan. Add the strips of steak to the pan and cook for 3 minutes, turning constantly.

2 Add the halved potatoes, diced carrot, sliced celery and leeks. Cook, stirring constantly, for a further 5 minutes.

3 Pour in the beef stock and bring to the boil over a medium heat. Reduce the heat until the liquid is simmering gently, then add the sliced baby corn cobs and the bouquet garni.

4 Cook the soup for a further 20 minutes or until the meat and all the vegetables are tender.

5 Remove the bouquet garni from the pan and discard. Stir the dry sherry into the soup and season to taste with salt and pepper.

6 Pour the soup into warmed soup bowls and garnish with the chopped fresh parsley. Serve immediately with crusty bread.

NUTRITION

Calories *187*; Sugars *3 g*; Protein *14 g*;
Carbohydrate *12 g*; Fat *9 g*; Saturates *2 g*

⭐⭐ easy
🕐 5 mins
🕐 35 mins

 COOK'S TIP

Make double the quantity of soup and freeze the remainder in a rigid container for later use. When ready to use, leave in the refrigerator to thaw thoroughly, then heat until piping hot.

Smoked haddock gives this soup a wonderfully rich flavour, while the mashed potatoes and cream thicken and enrich the stock.

Smoked Haddock Soup

1 Put the fish, onion, garlic and water into a pan. Bring to the boil, cover and simmer over a low heat for 15–20 minutes.

2 Remove the fish from the pan. Strip off the skin and remove all the bones and reserve both. Flake the flesh finely with a fork.

3 Return the skin and bones to the cooking liquid and simmer for 10 minutes. Strain, discarding the skin and bones. Pour the cooking liquid into a clean pan.

4 Add the milk and flaked fish and season to taste with salt and pepper. Bring to the boil and simmer for about 3 minutes.

5 Gradually whisk in sufficient mashed potato to give a fairly thick soup, then stir in the butter and sharpen to taste with lemon juice.

6 Add the fromage frais and 3 tablespoons of the chopped parsley. Reheat gently and adjust the seasoning if necessary. Sprinkle with the remaining parsley and serve immediately.

SERVES 4

225 g/8 oz smoked haddock fillet
1 onion, chopped finely
1 garlic clove, crushed
600 ml/1 pint water
600 ml/1 pint skimmed milk
225–350 g/8–12 oz hot mashed potatoes
25 g/1 oz butter
about 1 tbsp lemon juice
6 tbsp low-fat natural fromage frais
4 tbsp fresh parsley, chopped
salt and pepper

NUTRITION

Calories *169*; Sugars *8 g*; Protein *16 g*; Carbohydrate *16 g*; Fat *5 g*; Saturates *3 g*

easy

25 mins

40 mins

COOK'S TIP

Undyed smoked haddock may be used in place of the bright yellow fish; it will give a paler colour but just as much flavour. Alternatively, use smoked cod or smoked whiting.

Low-Fat Soups

Soups are traditional first course, but served with fresh crusty bread they can be a satisfying meal in their own right and – depending on the choice of ingredients – one that is low in calories. For the best results, use homemade stock from the liquid leftover from cooking vegetables and the juices from casseroles. Potatoes can also be added to the soup to thicken it instead of the traditional thickeners of flour or fat and water.

Serve this soup over ice on a warm summer day as a refreshing starter. It has the fresh tang of yogurt and a dash of spice from the Tabasco sauce.

Chilled Cucumber Soup

SERVES 4

1 cucumber, peeled and diced
400 ml/14 fl oz fresh fish stock, chilled
150 ml/5 fl oz tomato juice
150 ml/5 fl oz low-fat natural yogurt
150 ml/5 fl oz low-fat fromage frais
   (or double the quantity of yogurt)
125 g/4½ oz peeled prawns, thawed if frozen,
   roughly chopped
few drops Tabasco sauce
1 tbsp fresh mint, chopped
salt and white pepper
ice cubes, to serve

to garnish
sprigs of mint
cucumber slices
whole peeled prawns

1 Place the diced cucumber in a blender or food processor and work for a few seconds until smooth. Alternatively, chop the cucumber finely and push through a sieve.

2 Transfer the cucumber to a bowl. Stir in the stock, tomato juice, yogurt, fromage frais (if using) and prawns, and mix well.

3 Add the Tabasco sauce and season to taste.

4 Stir in the chopped mint, cover and chill for at least 2 hours.

5 Ladle the soup into glass bowls and add a few ice cubes. Serve garnished with mint, cucumber slices and whole prawns.

NUTRITION

Calories *83*; Sugars *7 g*; Protein *12 g*;
Carbohydrate *7 g*; Fat *1 g*; Saturates *0.3 g*

 very easy

3 hrs 30 mins

0 mins

 COOK'S TIP

Instead of prawns, add white crabmeat or minced chicken. For a vegetarian version of this soup, omit the prawns and add an extra 125 g/4½ oz finely diced cucumber. Use fresh vegetable stock instead of fish stock.

Whole young spinach leaves add vibrant colour to this unusual soup. Serve with hot, crusty bread for a nutritious light meal.

Yogurt *and* Spinach Soup

1 Pour the stock into a large pan, season and bring to the boil. Add the rice and simmer for 10 minutes or until barely cooked. Remove from the heat.

2 Combine the water and cornflour to a smooth paste. Pour the yogurt into a second pan and stir in the cornflour mixture. Set the pan over a low heat and bring the yogurt to the boil, stirring with a wooden spoon in one direction only. This will stabilise the yogurt and prevent it from separating or curdling on contact with the hot stock. When the yogurt has reached boiling point, stand the pan on a heat diffuser and simmer gently for 10 minutes. Remove the pan from the heat and set the mixture aside to cool slightly before stirring in the beaten egg yolks.

3 Pour the yogurt mixture into the stock, stir in the lemon juice and stir to blend thoroughly. Keep the soup warm, but do not allow it to boil.

4 Blanch the washed and drained spinach leaves in a large pan of boiling, salted water for 2-3 minutes or until they begin to soften but have not wilted. Tip the spinach into a colander, drain well and stir it into the soup. Warm through. Taste the soup and adjust the seasoning if necessary. Serve immediately in wide shallow soup plates, with hot, fresh crusty bread.

SERVES 4

600 ml/1 pint chicken stock
4 tbsp long-grain rice, rinsed and drained
4 tbsp water
1 tbsp cornflour
600 ml/1 pint low-fat natural yogurt
3 egg yolks, lightly beaten
juice of 1 lemon
350 g/12 oz young spinach leaves, washed and drained
salt and pepper
fresh crusty bread, to serve

NUTRITION
Calories 227; Sugars 13 g; Protein 14 g;
Carbohydrate 29 g; Fat 7 g; Saturates 2 g

 moderate

15 mins

30 mins

Tasty red lentil soup flavoured with chopped coriander is an easy microwave dish. The yogurt adds a light piquancy to the soup.

Red Lentil Soup *with* Yogurt

S E R V E S   4

25 g/1 oz butter
1 onion, chopped finely
1 celery stick, chopped finely
1 large carrot, grated
1 bay leaf
225 g/8 oz red lentils
1.2 litres/2 pints hot vegetable or chicken stock
2 tbsp chopped fresh coriander
4 tbsp low-fat natural yogurt
salt and pepper
fresh coriander sprigs, to garnish

1 Place the butter, onion and celery in a large bowl. Cover and cook in the microwave on High power for 3 minutes.

2 Add the carrot, bay leaf and lentils. Pour in the stock. Cover and cook on High power for 15 minutes, stirring halfway through.

3 Remove the bowl from the microwave oven, cover and stand for 5 minutes.

4 Remove and discard the bay leaf, then process in batches in a food processor, until smooth. Alternatively, press the soup through a sieve.

5 Pour the soup into a clean bowl. Season with salt and pepper to taste and stir in the coriander. Cover and cook on High power for 4–5 minutes or until piping hot.

6 Serve in warmed soup bowls. Stir 1 tablespoon of yogurt into each serving and garnish with small sprigs of fresh coriander.

N U T R I T I O N

Calories *280*; Sugars *6 g*; Protein *17 g*;
Carbohydrate *40 g*; Fat *7 g*; Saturates *4 g*

easy

5 mins

30 mins

 **C O O K ' S   T I P**

For an extra creamy soup try adding low-fat crème fraîche or soured cream instead of yogurt.

Thai soups are very quickly and easily put together, and are cooked so that each ingredient can still be tasted in the finished dish.

Mushroom *and* Ginger Soup

1 Soak the dried Chinese mushrooms (if using) for at least 30 minutes in 300 ml/½ pint of the hot vegetable stock. Remove the stalks and discard, then slice the mushrooms. Reserve the stock.

2 Cook the noodles for 2–3 minutes in boiling water. Drain and rinse. Set them aside.

3 Heat the oil over a high heat in a wok or large, heavy frying pan. Add the garlic and ginger, stir and add the mushrooms. Stir over a high heat for 2 minutes.

4 Add the remaining vegetable stock with the reserved stock and bring to the boil. Add the mushroom ketchup and soy sauce.

5 Stir in the bean sprouts and cook until tender. Put some noodles in each bowl and ladle the soup on top. Garnish with coriander leaves and serve immediately.

SERVES 4

15 g/½ oz dried Chinese mushrooms or 125 g/4½ oz field or chestnut mushrooms
1 litre/1¾ pints hot vegetable stock
125 g/4½ oz thread egg noodles
2 tsp sunflower oil
3 garlic cloves, crushed
2.5-cm/1-inch piece root ginger, shredded finely
½ tsp mushroom ketchup
1 tsp light soy sauce
125 g/4½ oz bean sprouts
coriander leaves, to garnish

 COOK'S TIP

Rice noodles contain no fat and are ideal for for anyone on a low-fat diet.

NUTRITION
Calories 74; Sugars 1 g; Protein 3 g; Carbohydrate 9 g; Fat 3 g; Saturates 0.4 g

✪✪　　　easy

　　　　1 hr 30 mins

　　　　15 mins

Carrot soups are very popular and here cumin, tomato, potato and celery give the soup both richness and depth.

Carrot *and* Cumin Soup

SERVES 4

40 g/1½ oz butter or margarine
1 large onion, chopped
1–2 garlic cloves, crushed
350 g/12 oz carrots, sliced
900 ml/1½ pints chicken or vegetable stock
¾ tsp ground cumin
2 celery sticks, sliced thinly
115 g/4 oz potato, diced
2 tsp tomato purée
2 tsp lemon juice
2 fresh or dried bay leaves
about 300 ml/ 10 fl oz skimmed milk
salt and pepper
celery leaves, to garnish

1 Melt the butter or margarine in a large pan. Add the onion and garlic and cook very gently until softened.

2 Add the carrots and cook gently for a further 5 minutes, stirring frequently and taking care they do not brown.

3 Add the stock, cumin, seasoning, celery, potato, tomato purée, lemon juice and bay leaves and bring to the boil. Cover and simmer for about 30 minutes or until the vegetables are tender.

4 Remove and discard the bay leaves, cool the soup a little and then press it through a sieve or process in a food processor or blender until smooth.

5 Pour the soup into a clean pan, add the milk and bring to the boil over a low heat. Taste and adjust the seasoning if necessary.

6 Ladle into warmed bowls, garnish each serving with a celery leaf and serve.

NUTRITION

Calories *114*; Sugars *8 g*; Protein *3 g*; Carbohydrate *12 g*; Fat *6 g*; Saturates *4 g*

easy

15 mins

45 mins

COOK'S TIP

This soup can be frozen for up to 3 months. Add the milk when reheating.

A traditional clear soup made from beef bones and lean minced beef. Thin strips of vegetables provide a colourful garnish.

Consommé

1 Put the stock and minced beef in a saucepan. Leave for 1 hour. Add the tomatoes, carrots, onion, celery, turnip (if using), bouquet garni, 2 of the egg whites, the crushed shells of 2 of the eggs and plenty of seasoning. Bring to almost boiling point, whisking hard all the time with a flat whisk.

2 Cover and simmer for 1 hour, taking care not to allow the layer of froth on top of the soup to break.

3 Pour the soup through a jelly bag or scalded fine cloth, keeping the froth back until the last, then pour the ingredients through the cloth again into a clean pan. The resulting liquid should be clear.

4 If the soup is not quite clear, return it to the pan with another egg white and the crushed shells of 2 more eggs. Repeat the whisking process as before, then boil for 10 minutes; strain again.

5 Add the sherry, if using, to the soup and reheat gently. Place the garnish in the warmed soup bowls and carefully pour in the soup. Serve with melba toast.

SERVES 4

1.25 litres/2¼ pints strong beef stock
225 g/8 oz extra lean minced beef
2 tomatoes, peeled, deseeded and chopped
2 large carrots, chopped
1 large onion, chopped
2 celery sticks, chopped
1 turnip, chopped (optional)
1 bouquet garni
2–3 egg whites
shells of 2–4 eggs, crushed
1–2 tbsp sherry (optional)
salt and pepper
melba toast, to serve

to garnish
julienne strips of raw carrot, turnip, celery or celeriac or a one-egg omelette, cut into julienne strips

NUTRITION
Calories *109*; Sugars *6 g*; Protein *13 g*; Carbohydrate *7 g*; Fat *3 g*; Saturates *1 g*

 challenging
 1 hr 15 mins
1 hr 15 mins

Special Occasion

The selection of soups in this chapter offers something a little different. Special occasion soups are appropriate for entertaining, either because of their festive ingredients or their suitability for an informal gathering, or perhaps because they require a little more preparation time than a family supper normally demands. The cold soups included in this chapter are also for special occasions and home entertainment, and are equally welcome on a hot summer's day as a refreshing treat.

Full of flavour, this rich and creamy soup is very simple to make and utterly delicious to eat.

Stilton *and* Walnut Soup

S E R V E S 4

60 g/2 oz butter
2 shallots, chopped
3 celery sticks, chopped
1 garlic clove, crushed
2 tbsp plain flour
600 ml/1 pint vegetable stock
300 ml/½ pint milk
150 g/5½ oz blue Stilton cheese, crumbled,
    plus extra to garnish
2 tbsp walnut halves, roughly chopped
150 ml/5 fl oz natural yogurt
salt and pepper
celery leaves, to garnish

1 Melt the butter in a large, heavy-based saucepan and sauté the shallots, celery and garlic, stirring occasionally, for 2–3 minutes or until they are softened.

2 Reduce the heat, add the flour and continue to cook, stirring constantly, for 30 seconds.

3 Gradually stir in the vegetable stock and milk and bring to the boil.

4 Reduce the heat to a gentle simmer and add the crumbled blue Stilton cheese and walnut halves. Cover and simmer for 20 minutes.

5 Stir in the yogurt and heat through for a further 2 minutes, but be careful not to let the soup boil.

6 Season the soup to taste with salt and pepper, then transfer to a warm soup tureen or individual serving bowls, garnish with celery leaves and extra crumbled blue Stilton cheese and serve at once.

N U T R I T I O N

Calories *392*; Sugars *8 g*; Protein *15 g*;
Carbohydrate *15 g*; Fat *30 g*; Saturates *16 g*

⭐ very easy
 10 mins
 30 mins

🍳 **C O O K ' S   T I P**

As well as adding protein, vitamins and useful fats to the diet, nuts add important flavour and texture to vegetarian meals.

Ground almonds add valuable protein and a rich, luxurious depth to this delicately coloured soup.

Carrot *and* Almond Soup

1 Heat the oil in a large saucepan over a medium heat and add the onion and leek. Cover and cook for about 3 minutes, stirring occasionally, until just softened; do not allow them to brown.

2 Add the carrots and water and season with a little salt and pepper. Bring to the boil, reduce the heat and simmer gently, partially covered, for about 45 minutes or until the vegetables are tender.

3 Soak the breadcrumbs in cold water to cover for 2–3 minutes, then strain them and press out any excess water.

4 Put the ground almonds and breadcrumbs in a blender or food processor with a ladleful of the carrot cooking water and purée until smooth and paste-like.

5 Transfer the soup vegetables and remaining cooking liquid to the blender or food processor and purée until smooth, working in batches if necessary. (If using a food processor, strain off the cooking liquid and reserve. Purée the soup solids with enough cooking liquid to moisten them, then combine with the remaining liquid.)

6 Return the soup to the saucepan and simmer over a low heat, stirring occasionally, until heated through. Add lemon juice, salt and pepper to taste. Ladle the soup into warmed bowls, garnish with chives and serve.

SERVES 4

2 tsp olive oil
1 onion, chopped finely
1 leek, sliced thinly
500 g/1 lb 2 oz carrots, sliced thinly
1.5 litres/2¾ pints water
50 g/1¾ oz soft white breadcrumbs
200 g/7 oz ground almonds
1 tbsp fresh lemon juice, or to taste
salt and pepper
snipped fresh chives, to garnish

NUTRITION
Calories *275*; Sugars *10 g*; Protein *9 g*; Carbohydrate *16 g*; Fat *20 g*; Saturates *2 g*

 moderate

15 mins

55 mins

A rich and creamy pale green soup made with avocados and enhanced by a touch of chopped mint. Serve chilled in summer or hot in winter.

Avocado *and* Mint Soup

SERVES 6

45 g/1½ oz butter or margarine
6 spring onions, sliced
1 garlic clove, crushed
25 g/1 oz plain flour
600 ml/1 pint vegetable stock
2 ripe avocados
2–3 tsp lemon juice
pinch of grated lemon rind
150 ml/5 fl oz milk
150 ml/5 fl oz single cream
1–1½ tbsp chopped mint
salt and pepper
mint sprigs, to garnish

minted garlic bread
125 g/4½ oz butter
1–2 tbsp chopped mint
1–2 garlic cloves, crushed
1 wholemeal or white French bread stick

NUTRITION
Calories *199*; Sugars *3 g*; Protein *3 g*;
Carbohydrate *7 g*; Fat *18 g*; Saturates *6 g*

⭐   very easy

🕐   15 mins

🕐   35 mins

1 Melt the butter or margarine in a large, heavy-based saucepan. Add the spring onions and garlic and cook over a low heat, stirring occasionally, for about 3 minutes or until soft and translucent.

2 Stir in the flour and cook, stirring, for 1–2 minutes. Gradually stir in the stock, then bring to the boil. Simmer gently while preparing the avocados.

3 Peel the avocados, discard the stones and chop coarsely. Add to the soup with the lemon juice and rind and seasoning. Cover and simmer for about 10 minutes or until tender.

4 Cool the soup slightly, then press through a strainer with the back of a spoon or process in a food processor or blender until a smooth purée forms. Pour into a bowl.

5 Stir in the milk and cream, adjust the seasoning, then stir in the mint. Cover and chill thoroughly.

6 To make the minted garlic bread, soften the butter and beat in the mint and garlic. Cut the loaf into slanting slices but leave a hinge on the bottom crust. Spread each slice with the butter and reassemble the loaf. Wrap in foil and place in a preheated oven at 180°C/350°F/Gas Mark 4 for about 15 minutes.

7 Serve the soup garnished with a sprig of mint and accompanied by the minted garlic bread.

This rich and elegant starter soup is perfect for a special dinner. The lobster shell, made into a stock, contributes greatly to the flavour of the soup.

Lobster Bisque

1 Pull off the lobster tail. With the legs up, cut the body in half lengthways. Scoop out the tomalley (the soft pale greenish-grey part) and, if it is a female, the roe (the solid red-orange part). Reserve these together, covered and refrigerated. Remove the meat and cut into bite-sized pieces; cover and refrigerate. Chop the shell into large pieces.

2 Melt half the butter in a large pan over a medium heat and add the lobster shell. Cook until brown bits begin to stick on the bottom of the pan. Add the carrot, celery, leek, onion and shallots. Cook, stirring, for 1½–2 minutes (do not let it burn). Add the alcohol and bubble for 1 minute. Add the water, tomato purée, a large pinch of salt and bring to the boil. Reduce the heat, simmer for 30 minutes and strain the stock, discarding the solids.

3 Melt the remaining butter in a small saucepan and add the tomalley and roe, if any. Add the cream, whisk to mix well and remove from the heat.

4 Put the flour in a small bowl and slowly whisk in 2–3 tablespoons of cold water. Stir in a little of the hot stock to make a smooth liquid.

5 Bring the remaining stock to the boil and whisk in the flour mixture. Simmer for 4–5 minutes or until the soup thickens, stirring frequently. Press the tomalley, roe and cream mixture through a sieve into the soup. Reduce the heat and add the lobster meat. Simmer gently until heated through.

6 Taste the soup and adjust the seasoning, adding more cream if wished. Ladle into warmed bowls, sprinkle with chives and serve.

SERVES 4

450 g/1 lb cooked lobster
45 g/1½ oz butter
1 small carrot, grated
1 celery stick, chopped finely
1 leek, chopped finely
1 small onion, chopped finely
2 shallots, chopped finely
3 tbsp brandy or Cognac
50 ml/2 fl oz dry white wine
1.2 litres/2 pints water
1 tbsp tomato purée
125 ml/4 fl oz whipping cream, or to taste
6 tbsp plain flour
salt and pepper
snipped fresh chives, to garnish

NUTRITION
Calories *398*; Sugars *6 g*; Protein *14 g*; Carbohydrate *30 g*; Fat *22 g*; Saturates *14 g*

 moderate

 20 mins

50 mins

This soup makes a rich and elegant starter. Serve it in shallow bowls so the oysters are visible, and make sure you warm the bowls to keep the soup hot.

Creamy Oyster Soup

SERVES 4

12 oysters
25 g/1 oz butter
2 shallots, chopped finely
5 tbsp white wine
300 ml/10 fl oz fish stock
175 ml/6 fl oz whipping or double cream
2 tbsp cornflour, dissolved in
　　2 tbsp cold water
salt and pepper
caviar or lumpfish roe, to garnish (optional)

NUTRITION
Calories *299*; Sugars *3 g*; Protein *3 g*;
Carbohydrate *16 g*; Fat *24 g*; Saturates *15 g*

　easy

　20 mins

　30 mins

1 To open the oysters, hold flat-side up, over a sieve set over a bowl to catch the juices, and push an oyster knife into the hinge. Work it around until you can prise off the top shell. When all the oysters have been opened, strain the liquid through a sieve lined with damp muslin. Remove any bits of shell stuck to the oysters and reserve them in their liquid.

2 Melt half the butter in a saucepan over a low heat. Add the shallots and cook gently for about 5 minutes until just softened, stirring frequently; do not allow them to brown.

3 Add the wine, bring to the boil and boil for 1 minute. Stir in the fish stock, bring back to the boil and boil for 3–4 minutes. Reduce the heat to a gentle simmer.

4 Add the oysters and their liquid and poach for about 1 minute or until they become firm but are still tender. Remove the oysters with a slotted spoon and reserve, covered. Strain the stock.

5 Bring the strained stock to the boil in a clean saucepan. Add the cream and bring back to the boil.

6 Stir the dissolved cornflour into the soup and boil gently for 2–3 minutes, stirring frequently, until slightly thickened. Add the oysters and cook for 1–2 minutes to reheat them. Taste and adjust the seasoning, if necessary, and ladle the soup into warmed bowls. Top each serving with a teaspoon of caviar or roe, if using.

This soup makes a festive seafood extravaganza worthy of a special celebration.

Bouillabaisse

1 Peel the prawns and reserve the shells. Cut the fish fillets into serving pieces about 5 cm/2 inches square. Trim off any ragged edges and reserve. Put the fish in a bowl with 2 tablespoons of the olive oil, the orange rind, 1 finely chopped garlic clove and chilli paste or harissa. Turn to coat well, cover and chill the prawns and fish separately.

2 Heat 1 tablespoon of the olive oil in a large saucepan over a medium heat. Add the leek, 1 onion, sliced and red pepper. Cover and cook for 5 minutes, stirring, until the onion softens. Stir in the tomatoes, remaining garlic cloves, sliced, bay leaf, saffron, fennel seeds, prawn shells, fish trimmings, water and fish stock. Bring to the boil, then simmer, covered, for 30 minutes. Strain the stock.

3 Heat the remaining oil in a large pan. Add the fennel and remaining onion, chopped finely, and cook for 5 minutes, stirring, until softened. Add the stock and potatoes and bring to the boil. Reduce the heat slightly, cover and cook for 12–15 minutes or until just tender.

4 Reduce the heat and add the fish, thick pieces first and thinner ones after 2–3 minutes. Add the prawns and scallops and simmer until all the seafood is cooked and opaque throughout.

5 Taste the soup and adjust the seasoning. Ladle into warmed bowls. Spread the aïoli sauce on the toasted bread slices and arrange on top of the soup.

SERVES 6

450 g/1 lb large prawns
750 g/1 lb 10 oz firm white fish fillets, such as sea bass, snapper and monkfish
4 tbsp olive oil
grated rind of 1 orange
5 large garlic cloves
½ tsp chilli paste or harissa
1 large leek, sliced
2 onions, halved
1 red pepper, deseeded and sliced
3–4 tomatoes, cored and cut into 8 wedges
1 bay leaf
pinch of saffron threads
½ tsp fennel seeds
600 ml/1 pint water
1.2 litres/2 pints fish stock
1 fennel bulb, chopped finely
225 g/8 oz potatoes, halved and sliced thinly
250 g/9 oz scallops
salt and pepper
toasted French bread slices and ready-prepared aïoli, to serve

NUTRITION

Calories 55; Sugars 1.1 g; Protein 7.2 g; Carbohydrate 2.6 g; Fat 1.8 g; Saturates 0.3 g

   easy

   10 mins

    1 hr

This tomato-based Californian soup is brimming with seafood, which can be varied according to availability. Serve it with olive bread or ciabatta.

Cioppino

SERVES 4

500 g/1 lb 2 oz mussels
500 g/1 lb 2 oz clams, rinsed
300 ml/10 fl oz dry white wine
1 tbsp olive oil
1 large onion, chopped finely
1 celery stick, chopped finely
1 yellow or green pepper, cored, deseeded
   and chopped finely
400 g/14 oz canned chopped tomatoes
   in juice
3 garlic cloves, chopped very finely
1 tbsp tomato purée
1 bay leaf
350 ml/12 fl oz fish stock or water
175 g/6 oz small squid, cleaned and
   cut into small pieces
225 g/8 oz skinless white fish fillets,
   such as cod, sole or haddock
150 g/5½ oz small scallops, or cooked
   shelled prawns
chopped fresh parsley, to garnish

NUTRITION
Calories *211*; Sugars *7 g*; Protein *26 g*;
Carbohydrate *10 g*; Fat *4 g*; Saturates *1 g*

 moderate

20 min

1 hr 15 mins

1 Discard any broken mussels and those with open shells. Rinse, pull off any 'beards', and scrape them with a knife under cold water. Put the mussels in a large heavy-based saucepan. Cover tightly and cook over a high heat for about 4 minutes or until the mussels open, shaking the pan occasionally.

2 Remove the mussels from the shells, adding any juices to the cooking liquid. Strain the cooking liquid through a muslin-lined sieve and reserve.

3 Put the clams into a heavy saucepan with 50 ml/2 fl oz of the wine. Cover tightly, place over a medium-high heat and cook for 2–4 minutes or until they open. Remove the clams from the shells and strain the cooking liquid through a muslin-lined sieve and reserve.

4 Heat the olive oil in a large saucepan over a medium-low heat. Add the onion, celery and pepper and cook for 3–4 minutes or until the onion softens, stirring occasionally. Add the remaining wine, tomatoes, garlic, tomato purée and bay leaf. Continue cooking for 10 minutes.

5 Stir in the fish stock or water, squid and reserved mussel and clam cooking liquids. Bring to the boil, reduce the heat and simmer for 35–40 minutes or until the vegetables and squid are tender.

6 Add the fish, mussels and clams and simmer, stirring occasionally, for about 4 minutes or until the fish becomes opaque. Stir in the scallops or prawns and continue simmering for 3–4 minutes or until heated through. Remove the bay leaf, ladle into warmed bowls and sprinkle with chopped parsley.

This lean, pretty soup makes an elegant light main course for 4 or it will serve 6 as a starter. Last-minute assembly is needed, but it's worth it.

Beef *and* Spring Vegetable Soup

1 Bring a pan of lightly salted water to the boil and add the potatoes and carrots. Reduce the heat, cover and simmer gently for about 15 minutes or until tender. Bring another pan of lightly salted water to the boil, add the beans and boil for about 5 minutes or until just tender. Drain the vegetables and reserve.

2 Bring the stock to the boil in a pan and add the soy sauce and sherry. Season with salt and pepper. Reduce the heat, add the beef and simmer gently for 10 minutes. (The beef should be very rare, as it will continue cooking in the bowls.)

3 Add the mushrooms and simmer for a further 3 minutes. Warm the bowls in a low oven.

4 Remove the meat and set aside to rest on a carving board. Taste the stock and adjust the seasoning, if necessary. Bring the stock back to the boil.

5 Cut the meat in half lengthways and slice each half into pieces about 3 mm/⅛ inch thick. Season the meat lightly with salt and pepper and divide between the warm bowls.

6 Drop the reserved vegetables into the stock and heat through for about 1 minute. Ladle the stock over the meat, dividing the vegetables as evenly as possible. Sprinkle over the parsley and chives and serve immediately.

SERVES 4 – 6

12 small new potatoes, quartered

4 slim carrots, quartered lengthways and cut into 4 cm/1½ inch lengths

150 g/5½ oz tiny French beans, cut into 4-cm/1½-inch lengths

1.5 litres/2¾ pints rich beef or meat stock

2 tbsp soy sauce

3 tbsp dry sherry

350 g/12 oz beef fillet, about 5-cm/ 2-inches thick

150 g/5½ oz shiitake mushrooms, sliced

1 tbsp chopped fresh parsley

1 tbsp chopped fresh chives

salt and pepper

NUTRITION

Calories *166*; Sugars *3 g*; Protein *16 g*; Carbohydrate *17 g*; Fat *4 g*; Saturates *1 g*

moderate

15–20 mins

35 mins

This soup needs a rich stock, and the mushrooms contribute plenty of extra flavour. The pastry top is baked separately to simplify serving.

Chicken *and* Mushroom Soup

SERVES 6

1.5 litres/2³⁄₄ pints chicken stock
4 skinless, boneless chicken breasts
2 garlic cloves, crushed
small bunch of fresh tarragon or
    ¹⁄₄ tsp dried tarragon
15 g/¹⁄₂ oz butter
400 g/14 oz chestnut or horse
    mushrooms, sliced
3 tbsp dry white wine
6 tbsp plain flour
175 ml/6 fl oz whipping or double cream
375 g/13 oz ready-rolled puff pastry
2 tbsp finely chopped fresh parsley
salt and pepper

NUTRITION
Calories 513; Sugars 2 g; Protein 28 g;
Carbohydrate 44 g; Fat 33 g; Saturates 10 g

⭐⭐⭐   moderate

    15 mins

    50 mins

1 Put the stock in a saucepan and bring just to the boil. Add the chicken, garlic and tarragon, reduce the heat, cover and simmer for 20 minutes or until the chicken is cooked through. Remove the chicken and strain the stock. When the chicken is cool, cut into bite-sized pieces.

2 Melt the butter in a large frying pan over a medium heat. Add the mushrooms and season with salt and pepper. Cook for 5–8 minutes or until they are golden brown, stirring occasionally at first, then stirring more often after they start to colour. Add the wine and bubble briefly. Remove from the heat.

3 Put the flour in a small mixing bowl and very slowly whisk in the cream to make a thick paste. Stir in a little of the stock to make a smooth liquid.

4 Bring the strained stock to the boil in a large saucepan. Whisk in the flour mixture and bring back to the boil. Boil gently for 3–4 minutes or until the soup thickens, stirring frequently. Add the cooked mushrooms and liquid, if any. Reduce the heat to low and simmer very gently, just to keep warm.

5 Cut out 6 rounds of pastry smaller than the soup bowls, using a plate as a guide. Put on a baking sheet, prick with a fork and bake in a preheated oven at 200°C/400°F/Gas Mark 6 for about 15 minutes or until deep golden.

6 Meanwhile, add the chicken to the soup. Taste and adjust the seasoning. Simmer for about 10 minutes or until the soup is heated through. Stir in the parsley. Ladle the soup into warmed bowls and place the pastry rounds on top. Serve immediately.

This an excellent soup to serve during the autumn, when pheasant are widely available.

Pheasant Soup *with* Cider

1 Melt half of the butter in a large saucepan over a medium heat. Add the shallots and garlic and cook for 3–4 minutes until softened. Pour over the cider and bring to the boil. Add the stock, carrot, celery, bay leaf and pheasant, which should be submerged. Bring back to the boil, reduce the heat, cover and simmer for about 1 hour or until the pheasant is very tender.

2 Remove the meat from the bones and cut into bite-sized pieces. Strain the stock, pressing with the back of a spoon to extract all the liquid. Discard the vegetables and bay leaf. Remove as much fat as possible from the stock.

3 Bring the pheasant stock to the boil in a large saucepan. Simmer gently. Add the potatoes and cook for about 15 minutes or until they are just barely tender.

4 Meanwhile, melt the remaining butter in a large frying pan over a medium heat. Add the mushrooms and season. Cook for 5–8 minutes until golden brown, stirring occasionally, then more often once they start to colour.

5 Add the mushrooms to the soup, together with the apple and cream, and cook for about 10 minutes or until the apple and potatoes are tender. Whisk the dissolved cornflour into the soup. Boil gently for 2–3 minutes, whisking, until slightly thickened. Add the pheasant meat and simmer gently until the soup is hot.

6 Heat the oil in a small frying pan until it starts to smoke. Add the sage leaves and fry for about 20 seconds or until crispy. Drain on paper towels. Ladle the soup into warmed bowls and garnish with fried sage.

SERVES 4

25 g/1 oz butter
3 shallots, chopped finely
2 garlic cloves, sliced thinly
300 ml/10 fl oz dry cider
1.2 litres/2 pints pheasant or chicken stock
1 carrot, chopped finely
1 celery stick, chopped finely
1 bay leaf
1 pheasant
300 g/10½ oz potatoes, diced
250 g/9 oz small button mushrooms, halved or quartered
1 large eating apple, peeled, cored and diced
300 ml/10 fl oz double cream
4 tbsp cornflour, dissolved with 3 tbsp cold water
salt and pepper

to garnish
2 tbsp olive oil, or as needed
30 sage leaves

NUTRITION
Calories 471; Sugars 8 g; Protein 12 g; Carbohydrate 32 g; Fat 32 g; Saturates 19 g

moderate

30 mins

1 hr 45 mins

If you can't find the preserved duck or goose (confit) that is traditionally used for this dish, you could braise duck legs in stock or substitute smoked chicken, but it will be a different soup.

Duck, Cabbage *and* Bean Soup

SERVES 6

2 preserved duck legs
1 tbsp duck fat or olive oil
1 onion, chopped finely
4 garlic cloves, chopped finely
2 carrots, sliced
1 large leek, halved lengthways and sliced
2 turnips, diced
200 g/7 oz dark leafy cabbage, such as cavolo nero or Savoy, sliced
1.2 litres/2 pints chicken or duck stock
2 potatoes, diced
225 g/8 oz dried white beans, soaked and cooked, or 800 g/28 oz canned white beans
1 bay leaf
2 tbsp roughly chopped fresh parsley
12 slices baguette
150 g/5½ oz grated Gruyère cheese
salt and pepper

NUTRITION
Calories *479*; Sugars *8 g*; Protein *29 g*; Carbohydrate *57 g*; Fat *16 g*; Saturates *7 g*

 easy
20 mins
1 hr 15 mins

1 Scrape as much fat as possible from the preserved duck. Remove the duck meat from the bones, keeping it in large pieces; discard the skin and bones.

2 Heat the duck fat or oil in a large soup kettle or flameproof casserole over a medium heat. Add the onion and three-quarters of the garlic. Cover and cook for 3–4 minutes or until just softened. Add the carrots, leek and turnips, cover and continue cooking for 20 minutes, stirring occasionally. If the vegetables start to brown, add a tablespoon of water.

3 Meanwhile, bring a large saucepan of salted water to the boil. Drop in the cabbage and boil gently for 5 minutes. Drain well.

4 Add the stock to the stewed vegetables. Stir in the potatoes, beans, parboiled cabbage and bay leaf, then adjust the seasoning. Bring almost to the boil, reduce the heat and simmer for 15 minutes.

5 Chop together the parsley and remaining garlic. Stir into the soup with the preserved duck, cover again and simmer for about 20 minutes, stirring occasionally. Season to taste.

6 Toast the bread under a preheated hot grill on one side. Turn and top with the cheese. Grill until the cheese melts. Ladle the soup into warmed bowls and top with the cheese toasts.

This delicious soup has a rich home-made Italian-style meat stock as a base. A perfect dinner party starter, it is very light – and easy to make if you have a supply of the stock in the freezer.

Parmesan Cheese Pancakes *in* Broth

1 To make the stock, put the meat in a large pot with the water, celery, carrot, onion, garlic, parsley stems, bay leaf and salt. Bring just to the boil and skim off the foam. Reduce the heat and simmer very gently, uncovered, for 2 hours.

2 Strain the stock and remove as much fat as possible. Discard the vegetables and herbs. (Save the meat for another purpose.)

3 Bring the stock to the boil in a clean saucepan. If necessary, boil to reduce the stock to 1 litre/1 ¾ pints. Taste and adjust the seasoning (be restrained with salt). Reduce the heat and simmer gently while making the pancakes.

4 To make the pancakes, put the flour in a bowl and add half the milk. Whisk until smooth, add the remaining milk and whisk again. Break in the eggs and whisk to combine well. Season and stir in the basil and Parmesan.

5 Brush the bottom of a small non-stick 15–18-cm/6–7-inch frying pan with oil and heat until it begins to smoke. Pour in one-third of the batter (about 4 tablespoons) and tilt the pan so the batter covers the bottom. Cook for about 1 minute or until mostly set around the edges. Turn the pancake and cook the other side for about 15 seconds. Turn out onto a plate. Continue making the remaining pancakes, adding more oil to the pan if needed.

6 Roll the pancakes up while warm, then cut into 3-mm/⅛-inch slices across the roll to make spirals. Divide the pancake spirals among bowls. Ladle over the hot broth and serve with Parmesan.

SERVES 4

1 tbsp plain flour
2 tbsp milk
2 eggs
2 tbsp chopped fresh basil
3 tbsp freshly grated Parmesan cheese, plus extra to serve
oil, to coat frying pan

meat stock

450 g/1 lb chicken wings and/or legs
250 g/9 oz lean boneless stewing beef, such as shin
1.4 litres/2½ pints water
1 celery stick, sliced thinly
1 carrot, sliced thinly
1 onion, halved and sliced
2 garlic cloves, crushed
3–4 parsley stems
1 bay leaf
½ tsp salt
pepper

NUTRITION
Calories 37; Sugars 0 g; Protein 3 g; Carbohydrate 3 g; Fat 2 g; Saturates 1 g

✪✪✪ moderate

25 mins

2 hrs 30 mins

This recipe uses the knobbly Jerusalem artichokes, which are curious to look at but taste delicious in a winter soup.

Artichoke *and* Swede Soup

SERVES 6

500 g/1 lb 2 oz Jerusalem artichokes
15 g/¹⁄₂ oz butter
1 onion, chopped finely
115 g/4 oz peeled swede, cubed
1 strip pared lemon rind
700 ml/1¹⁄₄ pints vegetable stock
3 tbsp double cream, plus extra to serve
1 tbsp fresh lemon juice, or to taste
4 tbsp lightly toasted pine kernels,
    to garnish

1 Peel the Jerusalem artichokes and cut the larger ones into pieces. Drop them into a bowl of cold water to prevent discoloration.

2 Melt the butter in a large saucepan over a medium heat. Add the onion and cook for about 3 minutes, stirring frequently, until just softened.

3 Drain the Jerusalem artichokes and add them to the saucepan with the swede and lemon rind. Pour in the stock, season with a little salt and pepper and stir to combine. Bring just to the boil, reduce the heat and simmer gently for about 20 minutes or until the vegetables are tender.

4 Allow the soup to cool slightly, then transfer to a blender or food processor and purée until smooth. (If you are using a food processor, strain off the cooking liquid and reserve. Purée the soup solids with enough cooking liquid to moisten them, then combine with the remaining liquid.)

5 Return the soup to the saucepan, stir in the cream and simmer for about 5 minutes or until reheated. Add the lemon juice. Taste and adjust the seasoning, adding more lemon juice if wished. Ladle the soup into warmed bowls and swirl in a little more cream, then very gently place the pine kernels on top, dividing them evenly. Serve at once.

NUTRITION
Calories *285*; Sugars *5 g*; Protein *5 g*;
Carbohydrate *16 g*; Fat *24 g*; Saturates *9 g*

moderate

20 mins

30 mins

The combination of potato, garlic and onion works brilliantly in soup. In this recipe the garlic is roasted to give it added depth.

Garlic *and* Potato Soup

1 Put the garlic in a baking dish, lightly brush with oil and bake in a preheated oven at 180°C/350°F/Gas Mark 4 for about 20 minutes or until golden.

2 Meanwhile, heat the oil in a large saucepan over a medium heat. Add the leeks and onion, cover and cook for about 3 minutes, stirring frequently, until they begin to soften.

3 Add the potatoes, roasted garlic, stock and bay leaf. Season with salt (unless the stock is salty already) and pepper. Bring to the boil, reduce the heat, cover and cook gently for about 30 minutes or until the vegetables are tender. Remove the bay leaf.

4 Allow the soup to cool slightly, then transfer to a blender or food processor and purée until smooth, working in batches if necessary. (If using a food processor, strain off the cooking liquid and reserve. Purée the soup solids with enough cooking liquid to moisten them, then combine with the remaining liquid.)

5 Return the soup to the saucepan and stir in the cream and a generous grating of nutmeg. Taste and adjust the seasoning, if necessary, adding a few drops of lemon juice, if desired. Reheat over a low heat. Ladle into warmed soup bowls, garnish with chives or parsley and serve.

SERVES 4

1 large head of garlic with large cloves, peeled (about 100 g/3½ oz)
2 tsp olive oil
2 large leeks, sliced thinly
1 large onion, chopped finely
500 g/1 lb 2 oz potatoes, diced
1.2 litres/2 pints vegetable stock
1 bay leaf
150 ml/5 fl oz single cream
freshly grated nutmeg
fresh lemon juice (optional)
salt and pepper
snipped fresh chives or parsley, to garnish

NUTRITION
Calories *240*; Sugars *7 g*; Protein *8 g*; Carbohydrate *33 g*; Fat *10 g*; Saturates *5 g*

✪✪✪   moderate

     10 mins

     1 hr

When cucumber is cooked it becomes a much more subtle vegetable, perfect to set off the taste of smoked salmon. This cold soup makes a lovely starter.

Cold Cucumber *and* Smoked Salmon Sou

SERVES 4

2 tsp oil
1 large onion, chopped finely
1 large cucumber, peeled, deseeded and sliced
1 small potato, diced
1 celery stick, chopped finely
1 litre/1¾ pints chicken or vegetable stock
150 ml/5 fl oz double cream
150 g/5½ oz smoked salmon, finely diced
2 tbsp chopped fresh chives
salt and pepper
fresh dill sprigs, to garnish

1 Heat the oil in a large saucepan over a medium heat. Add the onion and cook for about 3 minutes or until it begins to soften.

2 Add the cucumber, potato, celery and stock, along with a large pinch of salt, if using unsalted stock. Bring to the boil, reduce the heat, cover and cook gently for about 20 minutes or until the vegetables are tender.

3 Allow the soup to cool slightly, then transfer to a blender or food processor, working in batches if necessary. Purée the soup until smooth. (If using a food processor, strain off the cooking liquid and reserve it. Purée the soup solids with enough cooking liquid to moisten them, then combine with the remaining liquid.)

4 Transfer the puréed soup to a large container. Allow to cool completely, cover and refrigerate until cold.

5 Stir the double cream, smoked salmon and fresh chives into the soup. If time permits, chill for at least 1 hour to allow the flavours to blend. Taste and adjust the seasoning, adding salt, if needed, and pepper. Ladle into chilled bowls and garnish with dill.

NUTRITION
Calories 308; Sugars 7 g; Protein 13 g;
Carbohydrate 15 g; Fat 22 g; Saturates 12 g

easy

15 mins

25 mins

This brilliantly coloured soup makes a great summer starter, especially when peppers are abundant in farmers' markets – or in your garden.

Spicy Red Pepper Soup

1 Heat the oil in a large pan over a medium heat. Add the leeks, onion and garlic and cook, stirring occasionally, for about 5 minutes or until the onion is softened.

2 Stir in the peppers and cook for a further 2–3 minutes. Add the water, cumin, ground coriander and chilli purée with a pinch of salt. Bring to the boil, reduce the heat, cover and simmer gently for about 35 minutes or until all the vegetables are tender.

3 Set aside to cool slightly, then transfer to a blender or food processor and process to a smooth purée, in batches if necessary. (If using a food processor, strain off the cooking liquid and reserve. Purée the soup solids with enough cooking liquid to moisten them, then combine with the remaining liquid.)

4 Put the soup in a large bowl, then season with salt and pepper and add lemon juice to taste. Allow to cool completely, cover with clingfilm and chill in the refrigerator until cold.

5 Before serving, taste and adjust the seasoning, if necessary. Add a little more chilli purée if a spicy taste is preferred. Ladle into chilled bowls and garnish with spring onion greens or chives.

SERVES 6

1 tbsp olive oil
450 g/1 lb leeks, sliced thinly
1 large onion, halved and sliced thinly
2 garlic cloves, chopped finely or crushed
6 red peppers, deseeded and sliced
1 litre/1¾ pints water
½ tsp ground cumin
½ tsp ground coriander
1 tsp chilli purée
1–2 tsp fresh lemon juice
salt and pepper
spring onion greens, chopped finely, or fresh chives, to garnish

NUTRITION
Calories 90; Sugars 13 g; Protein 3 g; Carbohydrate 15 g; Fat 3 g; Saturates 0 g

⭐⭐⭐   moderate
        45 mins
        45 mins

The zingy hot taste of fresh ginger blends perfectly with cool melon in this delicious and intriguing soup.

Melon *and* Ginger Soup

SERVES 4

1 large ripe melon (about 1 kg/2 lb 4 oz)
¾ tsp grated peeled fresh root ginger, or to taste
1 tbsp fresh lemon juice, or to taste
1 tsp caster sugar
125 ml/4 fl oz whipping cream
salt
snipped fresh chives, to garnish

1 Halve the melon, discard the seeds and scoop the flesh into a blender or food processor. Purée until smooth, stopping to scrape down the sides as necessary to ensure no lumps remain. (You may need to work in batches.)

2 Add the grated ginger, lemon juice and sugar with a pinch of salt and process to combine. Taste and add a little more ginger, if liked. Scrape into a bowl, cover and chill completely for about 30 minutes or until cold.

3 Add the cream and stir to combine well. Taste and adjust the seasoning, adding a little extra salt and lemon juice if necessary.

4 To serve, divide the melon purée between four chilled bowls and garnish with chives.

NUTRITION

Calories *176*; Sugars *16 g*; Protein *2 g*; Carbohydrate *16 g*; Fat *12 g*; Saturates *7 g*

  moderate
  15 mins
   0 mins

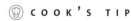 COOK'S TIP

To determine the ripeness of melon, gently press the end opposite the stem – it should 'give' a little, and there is usually a characteristic aroma on pressing that helps to confirm the verdict.

This soup brings together Thai flavours for a cool, refreshing starter. It highlights fresh coriander, now widely available.

Cold Coriander Soup

1 Heat the oil in a large pan over a medium heat. Add the onion, leek and garlic and cook, stirring occasionally, for 4–5 minutes or until the onion is softened, but not browned.

2 Add the water, courgette and white rice with a pinch of salt and some pepper. Stir in the lemon grass and lime leaves. Bring just to the boil and reduce the heat to low. Cover and simmer for 15–20 minutes or until the rice is soft and tender.

3 Add the fresh coriander leaves and stems, pushing them down into the liquid. Continue cooking over a low heat for 2–3 minutes or until the leaves are wilted. Remove and discard the lemon grass and lime leaves.

4 Remove from the heat and set aside to cool slightly, then transfer to a blender or food processor and process to a smooth purée, working in batches if necessary. (If using a food processor, strain off the cooking liquid and reserve. Purée the soup solids with enough cooking liquid to moisten them, then combine with the remaining liquid.)

5 Scrape the soup into a large container. Season to taste with salt and pepper. Allow to cool completely, cover with clingfilm and chill in the refrigerator until cold.

6 Taste and adjust the seasoning. For a spicier soup, stir in a little chilli purée to taste. For a thinner soup, add a small amount of iced water. Ladle into chilled bowls and garnish with finely chopped red pepper and/or chillies.

SERVES 4

2 tsp olive oil
1 large onion, chopped finely
1 leek, sliced thinly
1 garlic clove, sliced thinly
1 litre/1¾ pints water
1 courgette, about 200 g/7 oz, peeled and chopped
4 tbsp long grain white rice
5-cm/2-inch piece of lemon grass
2 lime leaves
55 g/2 oz fresh coriander leaves and soft stems
chilli purée, optional
salt and pepper
red pepper, chopped finely, and/or fresh red chillies, to garnish

NUTRITION
Calories 79; Sugars 5 g; Protein 3 g; Carbohydrate 13 g; Fat 3 g; Saturates 0 g

 easy

45 mins

30 mins

Index